JSCSC
LIBRARY
DATE 30/9/97
CLASS No.
355.81(41)HUN

Defending Northern Skies 1915 - 1995

24 October 1995

The Royal Air Force Historical Society at
The University of Newcastle

Edited by Air Vice-Marshal A F C Hunter CBE AFC DL

First published in the UK in 1996.

ISBN 0951 9824 6X

Typeset and printed in Great Britain by Fotodirect Ltd, Brighton

Royal Air Force Historical Society

Contents

Colonel The Viscount Ridley KG GCVO TD
Chancellor, University of Newcastle.

Foreword

Defending Northern Skies is the latest in a series of seminars organised by the Royal Air Force Historical Society, but the first to be held outside the Home Counties. In common with other major events run by the Society, an important objective of this seminar was to record the proceedings of the day, including the formal papers delivered by guest speakers and the contributions made by those present during discussion sessions.

Opening Remarks by Seminar Chairman, Air Vice-Marshal Sandy Hunter

It gives me great pleasure to welcome you all to this first major regional seminar arranged by the Royal Air Force Historical Society. I would extend a special welcome to Viscount Ridley, the Chancellor of Newcastle University and, through him, offer the Society's warm thanks to the Military Education Committee for their considerable moral and practical support. I am glad to see that a number of its members are present. I am also delighted to welcome a strong turnout from the Royal Air Force, headed by AVM Tony Bagnall, AOC 11 Group, and from his air defence stations at Boulmer, Buchan, Fylingdales, Leeming, Leuchars and Staxton Wold. It is good to see today's Defenders of Northern Skies out in force.

May I thank, in advance, all the speakers who, over a number of months, have responded to my blandishments and often intrusive guidance with great cheerfulness. I know that they have worked extremely hard to produce their papers. They bring great experience and insights to the Seminar. Coupled with them I would mention Philip Annis of the Royal Artillery Historical Trust who cannot be present but whose valuable paper on the AA defences of the North will be included in the published account of the day. Finally, I would pay tribute to the support of Air Cdre Ian Forster Director of the Department of Continuing Education at the University of Newcastle and to two members of his staff, Mrs Val Adams and Miss Caron Currie, whose efforts have produced the splendid administrative arrangements for the day.

In introducing the theme of the day, I would say that perhaps no single aspect of air power has a longer pedigree or shows greater continuity of principle than Air Defence. We can go back nearly 90 years in studying its evolution and we will begin our journey by looking at the threats that then were perceived to menace the UK, including these Northern Skies.

The Zeppelin Menace – Perceptions & Responses 1907-16

Chairman:

Professor Max HAMMERTON, Professor Emeritus of the Department of Psychology at the University of Newcastle began his Academic Career as a physicist and worked on the Blue Streak missile programme which he regards as having been from the outset a weapon of doubtful strategic value. He studied Applied Psychology at Cambridge where he earned a PhD. He came to Newcastle in 1973. He is a pillar of the Military Education Committee and is regarded as something of a cult figure by the undergraduate members of Northumbrian Universities Air Squadron

---

One of the most utterly obvious and at the same time extremely difficult things which must be done in any historical study is to keep ever in mind that nobody knew what was going to happen. When we find people of the highest intelligence worrying over things which did not, and, it seems in retrospect, could not have happened, we must remember that our past was still their hidden future. It is probable that none of us here today has ever seen a rigid airship: the last of them was broken up during the second world war. We tend to think of them as being as doomed as the dinosaurs; but in the early years of this century they loomed large in the thoughts of those interested in defence.

Although the Wrights had flown at thc end of 1903, the world at large remained ignorant of this – partly because of the brothers' own secretiveness – until Wilbur's triumphant visit to France in 1908. By this time scores of people had flown in a series of Zeppelin airships and their existence and supposed potential were very well publicised indeed. It may not be irrelevant that they were very impressive objects. Even the earliest were well over 100 metres long – you could have packed several Jumbos inside – and they went on growing. WWI types ranged from 150 to 200 metres in length with up to 60,000 cubic metres of gas.(1) It will not surprise anyone to learn that Dr Freud had his own suggestion to account for their newsworthy quality.

Neither was their actual performance contemptible. By the outbreak of war, DELAG, a subsidised company in Germany, had carried some thousands of passengers between various German cities without a single fatality, and flights of hundreds of kilometres were commonplace. A vehicle which could carry 20 passengers could evidently carry an equivalent weight of bombs, so there was some sound reason for concern. When H. G. Wells's The War in the Air appeared in 1908, it was seriously reviewed in Nature, amongst many less august journals, and was regarded as making entirely reasonable guesses. Those who have enjoyed this fascinating novel will recall that, in it, a fleet of 80-odd super-Zeppelin airships attacks and devastates New York, having destroyed a squadron of American battleships on the way over.

Quite serious reportage scarcely lagged behind. In 1909, American readers were assured that there would soon be 'Aerial Battleships' 400 metres long, with nose and tail turrets for 'big guns' and festooned with machine guns. Forty such ships, which could be built for the cost of but one Dreadnought, would suffice to conquer all Western Europe, and a mere half-dozen would be able to sink any surface ship.(2) Not long after, Lord Montagu of Beaulieu warned that 75 tons of bombs on the centre of London could bring the nation to its knees.

In the rather heated atmosphere created by such claims, especially in the context of increasing Anglo-German friction, it is not surprising that there were waves of nocturnal 'Zeppelin sightings' in 1912 and 1913, leading to questions being asked in Parliament. Ministers were justly sceptical, and it is indeed certain that no pre-war German airship flight approached anywhere near our coasts. Today, no doubt, whatever meteorological phenomena were so misinterpreted would be hailed as equally fictitious UFOs.

Nevertheless, airships did exist, aeroplanes were in the offing, and it behoved those responsible for the defence of the realm to think about them. Early in 1909 – i.e. before Bleriot's celebrated flight – the Committee of Imperial Defence ordered a sub-committee to look into the matter. Those who believe that pre-1914 official military thinking was reactionary and hidebound would do well to ponder the report that was produced.(3)

The sub-committee opined that, for the next few years at least, the principal use of aeroplanes would be for reconnaissance. Their load-carrying capacity was distinctly limited for offensive operations; and there was also the question of "the physical strain on the driver" – and if that sounds a trifle quaint, think of flying a Bleriot for a while.

They were distinctly more worried about airships. Not only was there their use as long-range naval reconnaissance machines, but they were expected to bomb both ships and dockyards. They might also transport "small raiding parties to attack special objectives" – a distant presage of the SAS! These possibilities had to be taken seriously. We know that, in 1914, Winston Churchill was concerned about the possibility of ships in the Thames being sunk at their moorings by Zeppelin attack; and he was never much given to panic.(4)

Old Admiral Wilson was largely disregarded when he predicted that airships would get quite lost trying to find their way around at night; and yet he was right. Taking star-sights with a misty horizon, and thence calculating position whilst unknown wind-drift was taking place proved to be the Devil's own job; and navigators were often wildly out in their reckoning. Remember that bubble-sextants and handy look-up tables did not yet exist – and even with them, as any WWII bomber crew will confirm, precision was more hoped-for than attained.

However, some precautions clearly needed to be taken. The War Office was not overly impressed by an offer to form a 'Volunteer Air Defence Force' made by an eccentric aircraft enthusiast named Pemberton-Billing. He claimed to be ready to lead a corps of owner-builder-flyers who would see off any marauding Zeppelins.(5) The proposed initial strength of this corps was five; but P-B's own aircraft proved unable to fly. (The frustrated patriot later became an MP, and some of his antics leave considerable doubts about his sanity.)

Nevertheless, the problem was seen as a real one. Rather surprisingly, it was thought that, although filled with thousands of cubic metres of hydrogen, Zeppelins would be very difficult to set alight.

The idea was widely held – I have been unable to track down its source – that German practice was to fill the space between the gas-bags and the envelope with inert engine-exhaust gases. In fact, it was not; although there is nothing wrong with the idea in principle; during WWII it was often Russian and, I understand, Japanese practice to bleed engine-exhaust into petrol tanks for precisely this purpose. Two ideas seemed reasonable: to drop small bombs upon them from aeroplanes (as Flt. Sub-Lt. Warneford later managed to do) and to destroy them with surface gunfire. The battleships commissioned in 1911, and subsequent classes, were fitted with a couple of 76.2mm AA guns – the letters standing for 'Airship Attacking'. It was a cloud no bigger than a man's hand.

The CID's sub-committee reported again in 1912. They were sceptical of an aeroplane's ability to defeat a Zeppelin, in view of the airship's 'great speed' (75 kph) and superior rate of climb; although they did not discount the idea entirely. They preferred the idea of airships fighting one another. The following year, the well-informed and semi-official Brassey's Naval Annual tended the other way, expecting 'torpedo-aeroplanes' to attack Zeppelins.[(6)] The usage is confusing: the writer did not mean aircraft carrying a torpedo, but ones hurling grenades at their targets, by analogy with the way in which destroyers were expected to try to torpedo battleships.

However, no man acquainted with inter-departmental politics will be in the least surprised to learn that one of the problems which immediately arose was: whose baby was it?

Again, remember the scale of the problem and the scant resources available. In August 1914, the Army and Navy had less than 120 aircraft between them, and far fewer AA guns. The Army demanded every one of its own for reconnaissance – and, be it added, made good use of them. There were hundreds of kilometres of coast, scores of ports, large and small, to defend and no experience to go on. Further, the traditional division of responsibilities between the Services made little sense in the new context.

Traditionally, the Navy's job was to prevent any enemy force approaching our coasts; whilst the Army was responsible for actual coast defence and the defeat of any bodies of troops which managed to evade the Navy and get ashore. Consistently, in August 1912, the RFC (I am using terminology which was only formalised later) was given the job of defending ports and other vital installations. It was the Navy, however, with Churchill urging, which established a string of coastal bases, intended to enable aircraft to co-operate with ships at sea. Thus, in November of 1913, whilst the RFC was still held responsible for home defence, the point defence of Naval bases was handed over to the RNAS.

In June the following year – remember again, no-one knew that 1914 was to be the year of reckoning – the matter was again under review. The Army reverted to the traditional position, and claimed sole responsibility. This was all very well; but the aircraft needed to undertake that responsibility simply did not exist; and when, a couple of months later, the BEF went to France, it took almost every serviceable machine in the RFC with it.

Thus it was more-or-less inevitable that, on the 5th of August, Churchill directed that the RNAS's first task was to meet enemy air attacks. On the 3rd September, after talks between Churchill and the War Minister, Lord Kitchener, the Cabinet formally decided that the Navy had responsibility for home defence. Churchill, of course, was never averse to responsibility; but the fact that the Navy had almost all the flyable aircraft left in Britain must have been at least as important as any personal factors.

After that, months passed without so much as a glimpse of a marauding Zeppelin in our skies. There were two main reasons for this: there were fewer available than was thought – only four at the date of the cabinet meeting just mentioned – and the German High Command – especially the Naval High Command – regarded them primarily as reconnaissance machines. The impulse to use them as strategic bombers came largely from middle-rank officers and enthusiasts.

It was not until the 3rd of January 1915 that a Zeppelin, itself hopelessly lost, entered our airspace. The inter-service squabblings, however, continued unabated. Churchill ceased to be First Lord of the Admiralty, and was succeeded by the far less dynamic Balfour on the 15th of May. In July, Balfour asked the Army to resume responsibility for the defence of London; and the War Office agreed to do so by the 1st of January 1916, subject to a string of confusing provisos.

Not all of the confusion was due to inter-service rivalries. No doubt Senior Officers enjoyed sniping at one another; but there was real uncertainty, both over what had been agreed and about the best method of attacking the raiders. Warneford's success in dropping bombs on one may well have misled the airmen; and their seniors clearly did not grasp that there were real problems in night flying.

Any modern pilot might care to look at the instrumentation available, and turn pale.

During the autumn, Zeppelin raids on London began; and it is no denigration of our forebears to say that there was a wave of panic and rage.[7] We have to remember the habit of impunity which the supremacy of the Navy had engendered, and the total novelty of the threat which looks so minor today. Partly as a sop to public opinion, the Government brought the eminent naval gunnery expert Sir Percy Scott out of retirement and made him responsible for the defence of London. Note: it was thought possible to treat London in isolation.

His first move was to bring guns sited at the coast inland and to demand 100 aircraft with highly qualified pilots. At the same time, Lord Kitchener, who cared little for agreements or formal organizations, ordered the RFC to deal with all air raids. Aircraft were duly moved to stations where they were likely to be able to intercept raiders; but they were few and rarely suitable.

Recriminations continued in an atmosphere of public outrage, continued failure to harm the raiders and a desperate shortage of equipment and trained personnel. Remember that the Western front was crying out for every aircraft it could get; and the generals could claim, not without justification, that the battlefield was decisive in a way the homeland was not. Also, the techniques of night flying were only slowly being mastered by a costly process of trial and error.

Nonetheless, some progress was being made. The first early warning devices – parabolic sound detectors – were being tested. A considerable administrative tidying-up was effected when the C in C Home forces finally took control during February 1916. A thoroughgoing scheme was planned, calling for 12 squadrons of specialised night fighters, 487 guns and 490 searchlights. Ninety-six airfields were prepared around the country and training was intensified. All the same, plans did not guarantee material. By June, less than half the planned numbers were available; but when a high-level conference was convened on the 14th of that month, the mood was distinctly more optimistic.[8]

BE2c and BE12 aircraft, whose inherent stability made them safer by night (although it made them terribly vulnerable to fighters in daylight over France) were in use. New weapons were under development: there were incendiary darts it was hoped to drop upon Zeppelins from above, recoilless guns for bombarding them from aircraft and three varieties of tracer rounds for machine-guns – which last were to prove, contrary to expectation, to be the most effective. Above all, there was, either in being or in preparation, a rational system for using what there was. Watchers at the coast, aided by listening devices, would warn airfields, withdrawn some tens of kilometres back to give time for the slow-climbing aircraft to reach combat height. (The listening devices were massive concrete affairs, some of which yet survive: there is one near Sunderland.[(9)]) Meanwhile, searchlights would try to illuminate the raiders, and a system of lighted patterns on the ground would give pilots at least a rough indication of where to search. (There were, remember, no radios light enough for aircraft to use.) Research had suggested that visual contact should be possible from about 600 metres, especially if the enemy were above the fighter. Meanwhile, the guns were concentrated around likely targets. A lull in attacks during the short summer nights gave a welcome space for training.

Early in the autumn, raids were resumed; and this time results were not long in coming. Around 0230 on the 3rd of September 1916, the SL 11 was shot down in flames by Lt. Leefe-Robinson. (I recall my mother telling me how she was called from her bed to see the flaming portent in the sky, and that a lot of people went to look for the wreckage in the morning, not realising that it was a dozen miles away.)

This was the beginning of the end. During the rest of 1916, a total of 29 Zeppelins crossed our coasts, of which 5 were destroyed. This was an unacceptable loss rate; and the German command called off their offensive. But at the end of November, C. G. Grey, the eccentric, rather unpleasant but highly acute editor of Aeroplane, warned his readers that "When the aeroplane raids start, and prove more damaging . . . the authorities cannot say that they have not had a fair warning."

Refs.

(1) See, e.g., Beaubois, H., *Airships* (London, Macdonald & Janes, 1973)

(2) Dienstbach, C. & MacMechan, T, In *McClure's Magazine* (N.Y., 1909)

(3) Cited in: Cole, C. & Cheesman, E., *The Air Defence of Great Britain, 1914-18* (London, Putnam, 1984) (This book is a 'must' for anyone interested in the subject.)

(4) See M. Gilbert's official biography, Vol. II, Ch.15.

(5) See Paris, M. The Amateur Military Tradition *J. Roy United Services Inst.*, Feb., 1993.

(6) *Brassey's Naval Annual, 1913* pp. 161 et seq.

(7) See, e.g., Aerial activities: the Murder Raiders &c., In: Hammerton, I., *The Great War Vol. IV* (London, Harmsworth, 1917)

(8) Cole et al., op. cit.

(9) AVM A F C Hunter, Personal Communication, 1995.

Air Defence against the Zeppelin – 1915-17

Chairman:

Robert JACKSON is a Yorkshireman, educated in Richmond and a resident of Darlington. In his time, he has been a pilot and navigation instructor and is now a full time historian, aviation writer and correspondent. He is a prolific writer and a great friend of the Society. In his first paper, he looks at the Zeppelin raids on the North of England in WWI and at the way in which the air defences of the North evolved in response to them.

Experimental in nature though they still were, the German Navy's Zeppelins were beginning to prove their worth in North Sea reconnaissance operations by the end of 1914, and a plan now formed to extend their role to offensive operations over the British Isles. The plan had actually originated some three weeks after the war began, but it had been shelved because the handful of Navy airships available during the last months of 1914 were fully committed to patrol and reconnaissance duties.

On 25 December 1914 the German Army used its small fleet of airships to raid the French towns of Nancy, Dunkirk and Verdun. The Navy immediately requested the release of its own airships to attack selected targets on the east coast of England, but the request was turned down by the Navy Minister, Grossadmiral von Tirpitz, who believed that the bombing of these targets by single airships would have little or no material effect. He advised Admiral Hugo von Pohl, the Chief of Naval Staff, to defer such a move until both Army and Navy were in a position to mount a maximum-effort raid on London with all available airships.

Another serious obstacle to the Navy's plans at this time was the Kaiser himself, who was unwilling to authorise the bombing of targets in Britain, and particularly in London. It all added up to frustration for the planning staff of the Naval Airship Division. By the middle of December the division had enough airships to carry out both the primary task of reconnaissance in co-operation with the High Seas Fleet and long-range special missions over England, and every delay in obtaining authority to undertake the latter type of operation meant that favourable weather conditions were being allowed to slip by. There was also the danger that the Navy's new airships might be destroyed in enemy air attacks before they could be used to good effect, and this fear was expressed in a letter to von Pohl from Konteradmiral Philipp, the Chief of German Naval Aviation. Pressure from Philipp and other senior naval commanders eventually resulted in von Pohl seeking an audience with the Kaiser on 7th January 1915, in which the admiral stressed the importance of attacking military objectives in England during the months of January and February, when weather conditions for long-range airship operations would be at their best.

Reluctantly, the Kaiser gave his consent to air attacks on the docks and military installations on the lower Thames and the east coast of England – but not on London. After months of waiting, the Airship Division could at last go ahead with its plan, already worked out in minute detail by Korvettenkapitan Peter Strasser, commanding the Naval Airship Division. The plan, submitted to von Pohl on 10 January 1915 for his final approval, envisaged attacks on Tynemouth, the Humber, Great Yarmouth, Lowestoft, Harwich and the Thames Estuary by three airships, which would bomb their targets at dusk after a daylight flight over the North Sea and return to their bases under cover of darkness.

The first attack, made on the night of 19/20 January 1915, was abortive in that no military targets were hit, although two airships penetrated into Norfolk and dropped their bombs in the vicinity of Great Yarmouth and King's Lynn, causing some £8,000-worth of damage and killing four people, one a small boy. Further attempts, made by Army airships during the next two months, were also abortive.

The North experienced its first Zeppelin attack on the night of 14/15 April 1915. Earlier, the naval airship L9, commanded by Kapitanleutnant Heinrich Mathy, had set out on a reconnaissance flight to the west of Terschelling. She carried ten 110lb. high explosive and 40 incendiary bombs, and after flying all day without sighting any British ships, Mathy obtained permission to carry out a raid on a British coastal target before returning to base. The objective selected by Mathy was Tynemouth, with its complex of shipyards, but landfall was made at Blyth, some miles to the north, and the L9's commander mistook the Wansbeck for the Tyne. Most of his bombs fell harmlessly in open country around the area's mining villages, although two people were injured at Wallsend when a near-miss damaged their house. Convinced that he had inflicted considerable damage on the Tyne's shipyards, Mathy set course for home. A solitary Bristol TB8 took off from the Royal Naval Air Station at Whitley Bay, established six weeks earlier to counter Zeppelin attacks on the Tynemouth area, and patrolled at 5,000 feet over Newcastle for an hour, unassisted by any searchlights and without sighting the enemy.

At this time the air defence of Great Britain was the sole responsibility of the Royal Naval Air Service, mainly because the RNAS had more aircraft available than the Royal Flying Corps. Most of the naval aircraft assigned to air defence, however, were concentrated in the home counties and East Anglia, as were the relatively few anti-aircraft guns and searchlights, so that the North's defences were minimal. The Whitley Bay station, for example, had three aircraft (two of which were unserviceable) at the time of the L9's incursion, and its weaponry comprised a few carbines with 209 incendiary rounds between them, 24 Hale rifle grenades without the rifles to fire them, and twenty Hale incendiary bombs with only one set of dropping gear.

On the night of 6 June Heinrich Mathy's L9 was once again active over the north, and this time the target was Hull. The Zeppelin dropped ten HE and 50 incendiary bombs, killing 24 people, injuring 40, and causing nearly £45,000-worth of damage. Naval aircraft took off from Killingholme and Yarmouth, but failed to make contact. Three Army Zeppelins which set out to raid London on this night failed to reach the English coast for various reasons, and one of them,

LZ37, was destroyed over Belgium by Flight Sub-Lt Reginald Warneford, flying a Morane Parasol, who dropped six 20lb bombs on it after a chase lasting an hour. The encounter was accidental, as Warneford had been en route to attack the airship shed at Berchem Ste Agathe, but it proved that the Zeppelin was vulnerable to air attack provided the attacking aircraft had the advantage of height. In this case Warneford, who coaxed his Morane up to 11,000 feet, sighted the airship as it was passing through 7,000 feet, descending towards its base at Evere. A second Airship, LZ38, was destroyed soon after docking at Evere when its shed was bombed by pilots of No. 1 RNAS Squadron, based in France.

Following the loss of the two Army ships a tentative plan by the Navy to position its own airships at forward bases in Belgium was abandoned, and the next raid on Britain was made from Nordholz on the night of 15 June by the L10 commanded by Kapitanleutnant Hirsch. The L10 was an improved type of Zeppelin and was the forerunner of nine more airships of a similar class, all with a capacity of 1,126,000 cubic feet, which would be bought by the Navy before the end of 1915. The ships were 536 feet long and were powered by four 210hp Maybach engines. They could cruise at 11,000 feet and fly as far as the west coast of England with a two-ton bomb load.

The L10's target on this June night was Tyneside. Hirsch crossed the coast near Blyth at a quarter to midnight, turned south, and for half an hour dropped 3,500lb of bombs on Wallsend, Jarrow and South Shields, killing eighteen people, injuring 72 and causing damage amounting to nearly £42,000. No warning of the raid had been received, and much of the target area was brightly lit. Two sorties by BE2 aircraft were flown from Whitley Bay, but no contact was made. As a result of this raid, the Tyneside garrison commander advised Major-General H M Lawson, the GOC-in-C Northern Command, that the naval aircraft at Whitley Bay were inadequate for the defence task, and that an additional air station at Gosforth would be an advantage. The recommendation was approved, and a small RNAS detachment under Lieutenant Christopher Draper was operational there in July.

The next attack on the North, on the night of 9 August, was intended as a diversion for a major raid on London, which in the event was a dismal failure. The northern raider was once again the old L9, commanded this time by Kapitanleutnant Odo Loewe, who crossed the coast near Hornsea and bombed Goole in the belief that it was

Hull. Air defence sorties were flown from Hornsea racecourse, Redcar – where there was a naval flying training establishment – and Whitley Bay, but although the L9 was sighted by pilots from Hornsea she was not engaged and escaped in thick mist.

Odo Loewe and the L9 returned to the north on the night of 8 September, crossing the coast near Whitby at 9.15 to raid the iron-works at Skinningrove. The attack was made with great accuracy but little damage was done, and the Zeppelin was well clear of the area before the first aircraft – a BE2 from Redcar — arrived on the scene. This was the last attack made on the North in 1915, and raids on southern England petered out a month later. For the remaining weeks of the year, the Navy's Zeppelins were either employed on co-operation work with the Fleet or were grounded by bad weather. When operations began again in January 1916, they were directed against targets spread along the whole length of England. The first raid of the year, on the last night of January, was a deep-penetration mission against Liverpool by nine Zeppelins. Twenty-two air defence sorties were flown without result, but one airship, the L19, came down in the North Sea through a combination of engine trouble and rifle fire from the Dutch Friesian Islands and was lost with all her crew, including her commander, Odo Loewe.

During 1915, it had become increasingly apparent that the Navy was ill-equipped to deal with the Zeppelin threat, and it was clear that if matters were to improve the Royal Flying Corps, which had assisted the RNAS to a limited extent in the course of the year, would have to become much more involved, even to the extent of assuming the air defence commitment in full. The Admiralty and the War Office, however, found it hard to agree on anything, beyond the fundamental facts that Zeppelins were difficult to find in the dark and that night flying was fraught with peril, so while very brave young men in wholly inadequate aircraft were striving to confront the enemy, another war was being waged in Whitehall – a prolonged and unseemly wrangle over the responsibility for Britain's air defence.

In June 1915, the Director of Home Defence, General Launcelot Kiggell, had proposed that the Navy deal with enemy aircraft approaching the coast and that the Army take over once the enemy had come inland; this was firmed up by the Army Council in November, but it was not until 10 February 1916 that a formal agreement to this effect was endorsed by the War Committee. With effect from 12 noon on 16 February, 1916, the Commander-in-Chief Home

Forces was to assume responsibility for the defence of London, and for the rest of the country on the 22nd.

Meanwhile, by prior agreement with the RNAS, the RFC had positioned three BE2cs at Cramlington on 1 December 1915 for the defence of Tyneside, and on 18 March 1916 these formed the nucleus of the newly-formed No. 36 Squadron, the first RFC squadron formed for the specific task of home defence. Flights were quickly established at Ashington, Hylton and Seaton Carew. Later in March, for the air defence of the southern part of the region, No. 33 Squadron was transferred from Filton to Beverley in Yorkshire, with a detached flight at Bramham Moor, Tadcaster. In September 1916 No. 76 Squadron formed at Ripon, with detached flights at Copmanthorpe, Helperby and Catterick, and in the following month No. 77 Squadron became established at Edinburgh, with flights at Whiteburn, New Haggerston and Penston. By the end of the year, therefore, the North was defended by four front-line squadrons, all equipped with BE2 and, later, BE12 aircraft. Between them they had at their disposal no less than 34 landing grounds between Humber and Tyne and 35 between Tyne and Forth.

Despite these deployments, no raider was destroyed by the northern air defences in the course of seven attacks that were made on targets from the Forth to the Humber between the beginning of March and the end of September 1916. Deployment of anti-aircraft weaponry to the North was still painfully slow, and it took a particularly costly raid on Hull on the night of 5 March 1916, after which a mob smashed up a vehicle belonging to the RFC, to bring about the hasty installation of two 13-pounder, two three-inch, one 12-pounder and one 6-pounder gun, while at the same time the defences around the Humber and along the east coast were generally strengthened.

While the RFC strove to achieve some form of effective night defence organization, a warning system was established and observer posts set up all over the country. These were connected with warning control centres and gradually began to prove their worth. Girls' names were used to identify individual Zeppelins, which were listed in alphabetical order as they crossed the coast. One of the first lines of defence against the incoming Zeppelins was the interception of their wireless traffic by direction-finding stations such as that at Stockton-on-Tees, and by the end of 1916 a network of huge sound locator mirrors, some built into cliffs, had also been set up. Three can still be seen, at Boulby near Skinningrove, Marske by Redcar, and Fulwell just North of Sunderland.

By August 1916 the squadrons of the Home Defence Wing had adopted a system whereby aircraft operating from the 69 landing grounds in the North were assigned individual patrol areas which overlapped, so that if a Zeppelin was sighted mutual support was readily available – at least in theory. Although aircrews had now amassed a considerable amount of experience in night operations, and were aware that night flying held no special complications, the Zeppelins remained notoriously hard to locate without searchlight assistance, anti-aircraft shellbursts or marker rockets, the latter fired by the coastal observers.

Then there was the problem of armament. Time does not permit a full appraisal of what was available up to the summer of 1916; suffice to say that it was necessary for a fighter pilot to manoeuvre his aircraft into position above an airship in order to drop his incendiary bombs and explosive darts on it. The problem here was that, because of the Zeppelin's superior rate of climb, it was often difficult, if not impossible, for the attacking aircraft to climb above it. The answer, clearly, was to be able to attack from any position, including below, using explosive bullets.

Such bullets had existed for some years. One had been invented by a New Zealander, John Pomeroy, in 1908 and had been offered without success to the British government in 1914; it was only in 1916, after Pomeroy had written to David Lloyd George, that the Munitions Inventions Department agreed to sponsor development. In August that year, an order for half a million rounds was placed on behalf of the RFC.

The Admiralty had shown more interest in an explosive bullet designed by Flight Lieutenant F. A. Brock, and this was also ordered for both the RNAS and RFC, as was a phosphorus incendiary bullet designed by a Coventry engineer, J. F. Buckingham. This mixture of bullets was on issue to the home defence squadrons by the end of August 1916.

The result was immediate, and dramatic. On the night of 2 September, the Army's Schutte-Lanz airship SL11 (Hauptmann Wilhelm Schramm) was shot down in flames at Cuffley by Lieutenant William Leefe Robinson of No. 39 Squadron. On 22 September L32 (Oberleutnant-zur-See Werner Peterson) fell in flames over Esscx after being attacked by 2nd Lieutenant Frederick Sowrey, while Alois

Bocker's L33 crash-landed near Little Wigborough having suffered severe damage from anti-aircraft fire and the efforts of Lieutenant Alfred Brandon of 39 Squadron. Finally, on 1 October, one of a force of eleven Zeppelins that set out to raid England was shot down over Potters Bar by 2nd Lt. W. J. Tempest. She was the L31, commanded by Heinrich Mathy.

All these successes had been in the South. But on the night of 28/29 November the northern air defences at last had their chance. Zeppelin L34, Kapitanleutnant Max Dietrich, was shot down off the coast by 2nd Lieutenant Ian Pyott of No. 36 Squadron, flying a BE2c from Seaton Carew, soon after bombing targets in south-east Durham. All twenty crew perished. Another airship, the L21, was also destroyed that night by naval pilots from Great Yarmouth.

The Zeppelins were to make three more attacks on the North before the end of the war, but the raids were of little significance. From May 1917, the emphasis switched to attacks on London and the South-east by heavier-than-air bombers; and it may be said with justification that the ascendancy of the Zeppelin ended for good when Max Dietrich's L34 fell to the guns of Ian Pyott over Hartlepool Bay on that November night in 1916.

Air Defence in the North – The Air Defence System

Chairman:

After WWI, there occurred one of these difficult situations in which military men could point to no definite threat in order to justify expenditure on Defence. Not for the last time, the politicians had a field day! I recall being told by one of the RAF's great wartime leaders, Sir Hugh Constantine, that in 1928, serving on his first fighter squadron, he went to his flight commander and asked: 'Sir, who is our enemy?' The flight commander thought for a moment and replied: 'You silly young man (or words to that effect), it's the French!' It was in that climate that, amazingly, the Dowding System was born, a system which might be said in the terms of the stud book to be 'by Watson-Watt out of Ashmore'.

There is nobody better equipped to tell that story than Derek WOOD. Co-author of The Narrow Margin, and historian of the ROC, Derek Wood is a distinguished aviation correspondent and founder of Jane's Defence Weekly. He is also a stalwart member of the committee of the RAF Historical Society.

The essential elements of any air defence system, in relation to the threat, have been the same since World War I. The defence has to know What is it? Where is it? Where is it going? Inevitably a sub-question is, what can we do about it? Air defence of the North of Britain has been no exception to these rules. The level of urgency to get the questions answered has, of course, depended on whether you believed the encmy could reach you. As long as it was felt that you were out of range, then you were afforded the luxury of relaxing and writing suitable staff papers.

The first man to appreciate the need to answer the basic questions and keep the answers visually up-dated on a situation display was not an RAF Commander but a Gunner, Major General E. B. Ashmore. He was, in fact, the father of all modern air defence systems – although he never received the real recognition that was due to him.

Ashmore, who had learned to fly and wore a Royal Flying Corps pilot's wings, built the London Air Defence Area (LADA for short) in 1917-18. Out of chaos he produced a standardised system of reporting for all defence units which passed information on a basic grid to the operations map table in his headquarters. He was then able to direct the means of defence.

The great benefits of his layout and methods were that they could be expanded to cover much larger areas of the country. Ashmore was a formidable man to meet – as I discovered as a youngster in the summer of 1940, when he was commanding the newly formed 6th Battalion of the West Sussex Home Guard.

After World War I, LADA and virtually all vestiges of air defence disappeared in a wave of peace euphoria. It was not until 1924 that the Committee of Imperial Defence formed a sub-committee under Major General Romer to study air defence. Remarkably, this happened because of a possible threat from France which had retained a sizeable air force, while we had hacked ours to pieces. It was accepted by the sub committee that "the civil population will be so vitally affected by air attacks that the responsibility for observation and warning cannot be considered exclusively military". How prophetic that was!

Ashmore was a member of that sub-committee and, in August and September 1924 he organised a programme of aircraft observation and tracking experiments in Kent. The observers at nine posts were Special Constables recruited by the Home Office and they reported to an Ashmore-type operations room in Cranbrook Post Office. Excellent results were obtained by using a Sopwith Snipe fighter of No. 32 squadron. Ashmore was then requested to set up the Observer Corps with an initial two groups, with operations rooms or centres at Maidstone and Horsham. At the time he could little have thought that the volunteers would eventually become the Royal Observer Corps covering England, Scotland and Wales and operating day and night through five and a half years of war.

The slump and shortage of cash meant that various schemes for improving air defence did not get put into operation – which, of course, is nothing new! The emergence of Nazi Germany as a major air power in the '30s altered everything. The increasing range of bombers meant that at 350 miles radius from Germany, an area up to just south of the Tees was threatened.

The Observer Corps was an overland human sensor, using eyes and ears. An air defence system, however, is only as good as its long range sensors; without early warning, interceptors cannot be positioned in time to be effective. The only alternative, up to the late nineteen-thirties, was standing patrols – wasteful and largely ineffective.

In World War I, sound detectors were used with varying degrees of success. Indeed, the earliest surviving examples are in the North, with one of 1916 vintage marooned on a housing estate in Redcar and another, probably of the 1920's in a field at Kilnsea. The Army laboured long and hard on sound mirrors, as they were called, the ultimate being a 1929 200ft. concrete arc still in existence, along with other smaller variants, in Kent. The overall problems were short range, difficulty in operation and susceptibility to every kind of noise interference.

Abruptly, in 1935, the whole scene changed and the vast sound locators became as outdated as the dinosaurs. On the 26th February in that year, Robert Watson-Watt and his small team from the Radio Research Station at Slough demonstrated that short wave radio pulses could be reflected from an aircraft and the measurable return displayed on a cathode ray tube.

With remarkable speed the invention was developed into RDF (Radio Direction Finding) – a name designed to confuse the enemy as to its purpose. The name Radar came later but I will use it here as it is more familiar. In September 1935 the decision was taken to build a chain of 20 CH (Chain Home) RDF stations from the Tyne to Southampton with an initial five stations covering the Thames Estuary. The first station was set up at Bawdsey where most of the experimental work was carried out.

Meanwhile, in 1936 the operational layout of the Metropolitan Air Forces underwent a radical change, with the setting up of Fighter, Bomber and Coastal Commands. It was very fortunate indeed that the first Commander-in-Chief of Fighter Command should be Sir Hugh, later Lord, Dowding. He understood the need for applying science and engineering to air defence.

Through the second half of the thirties the East and South Coast radar chains were gradually taking shape despite every sort of problem, not least the supply of equipment. From 1937 it was agreed that the Humber, Tees, Tyne and Forth should have radar coverage of the highest quality available and this programme was accelerated at the time of the Munich crisis in 1938. To cover the Tyne, a mobile set was put up at Ravenscar and another for the Forth-Clyde area at Drone Hill. These were later superseded by permanent stations. Thus the North, with its vital naval, shipping and shipbuilding resources was put on the same footing as the South. In 1939 the coverage was extended to the Fleet anchorage at Scapa Flow.

To cope with low level raiders which could fly in below 5,000ft. and under the CH station's view, a radar known as Chain Home Low, or CHL for short, was developed and entered service late in 1939. Behind the radar chain, Observer Corps groups had to be formed, recruited and equipped as there was no radar view overland. The Home Office was pressing for nationwide Observer Corps coverage to ensure that basic civil defence measures would work.

The years 1936 to 1940 saw a continuous expansion of the Observer Corps with five areas set up, including Northern and Scottish, their respective headquarters being at Catterick and Edinburgh. Within these areas, Group operations rooms and posts were established. By the summer of 1940 most of Britain was covered except for West Wales and part of Cornwall.

The posts plotted, with a rudimentary but effective instrument, their reports going direct to an Observer Group ops room, which, in turn, relayed the reports from its table to the fighter Group. In addition observer groups had a direct line to a Sector Station. Coastal observer groups later had a "Sea Plotter" who received radar information told from Group. As in all the RAF operations rooms, the Observer Corps had a synchronised colour clock used in conjunction with coloured counters and plaques. When a particular colour appeared, stale information on the table would be removed.

For the control and reporting organisation to work and not just produce a mass of unco-ordinated information on which interception instructions were impossible, other steps had to be taken. Interception trials at Biggin Hill were carried out in 1936-37. After endless hours of calculators and mathematics the simple solution occurred to the Station Commander, Wing Commander Grenfell. Based on an isosceles triangle, he visualised the changing situation using that remarkable instrument the human eye and he got a perfect interception.

Squadron Leader (later Air Marshal Sir) Raymund Hart, started the world's first radar training school at Bawdsey and also developed a filter room there. This analysed and cleaned up the radar information before it was committed to plot. The filter room was later transferred to Bentley Priory and provided the clean picture on the main table at Fighter Command.

In addition, complex communications, including the Defence Teleprinter Network had to be provided. To get aircraft back to base, high frequency direction finding (HF/DF) was used, while a device known as "Pip Squeak" was installed on fighters so that they could transmit automatically at set intervals for a fix, using HF/DF. Great efforts were made to provide VHF/RT for ground/air communications in place of HF with which there were increasing technical problems. In the event, time was against us and it was not until the end of September 1940 that a suitable VHF set was available in quantity.

Another key element was the 'Y' service. The long range stations read and analysed Luftwaffe WT traffic and gave very useful intelligence on order of battle and impending operations. From the spring of 1940 we also had very effective stations on HF/VHF bands which listened in to German RT traffic. At the Battle of Britain stage Ultra, for a variety of reasons, played very little direct part despite some of the fanciful writing on the subject.

A continuous programme of exercises and product improvement was to go on right through the summer of 1940. By spring of that year the basic layout was in place with Nos. 11, 12 and 13 Fighter Groups occupying underground operations rooms at Uxbridge, Watnall and Newcastle respectively. Nos. 9, 10 and 14 Groups became operational later in the year. Within the groups, the Sector Operations Rooms controlled the fighters. Radar information was relayed directly to Bentley Priory, filtered and told down to Groups.

Three flights in 1939 are worthy of mention at this point as they had a major effect on the system. These were the electronic reconnaissance sorties of the airship Graf Zeppelin. Equipped with high grade radio receivers, the airship cruised up the East coast to see whether the giant British masts were transmitting. The flights moved up past the CH stations, one getting as far as Scapa Flow. The result was nothing but a deafening hum which drove the operators mad. They assumed that it was probably a leak from the 50Hz British

National Grid and that the RAF was not operating radar. The most likely answer was that the German receivers were being jammed by the 50Hz transmissions of the CH stations themselves with the vast airship envelope amplifying the noise.

The Germans were developing radar at much shorter wavelengths and higher frequency and assumed that the 10-13.5m wavelength of CH was pretty well unusable. Thus, when the Battle of Britain started, the Luftwaffe had a great technical shock and tried, largely unsuccessfully, to produce jamming equipment in a hurry and they spasmodically attacked the radar sites, on one or two occasions with considerable success. Into the gaps thus caused we put mobile equipment, so the German listeners assumed the stations were still transmitting.

Coming to the war itself, the first major attack on this country on October 16, 1939, could not be considered an outstanding success from the air defence point of view, as the radar involved suffered a power failure at the crucial moment.

Nine of the then new Ju88s of KG30 put in a surprise attack on the Firth of Forth, damaging two cruisers and a destroyer. Nos. 602 and 603 Squadrons succeeded in getting to them and shot down two with a further two damaged. The sirens sounded late and the gun operations room was confused – with the result that guns fired too late or not at all. The Observer Corps acquitted itself well and was rewarded with a message of commendation from Dowding. The next day KG30 attacked Scapa Flow severely damaging the old depot ship Iron Duke.

It was not until October 28th, however, that the first Luftwaffe aircraft was brought down overland. A Heinkel 111, it crashed near Humbie, East Lothian. Reconnaissance, minelaying and convoy attacks were the main sources of enemy incursion in the "Phoney War" months up to the Battle of Britain.

On August 15th, 1940, one of the most important days of the Battle occurred. The system in the North East had its greatest test and was not found wanting. The Luftwaffe decided that most of the RAF strength had gone South to reinforce the hard pressed squadrons and that an attack in the North East on airfields would be a walkover, while the South was under heavy pressure. They therefore threw the full weight of Luftflotte 5 in Norway into the fray. Two units of Heinkel 115 seaplanes departed for Dundee to act as a "spoof" to draw any fighters off. These were apparently seen by the CHL radar at Anstruther which alerted the system. However, the main force, consisting of 63 Heinkel 111s and 21 Messerschmitt 110s acting as escort, made a major navigational error which brought them in close and parallel to the seaplanes.

On realising its mistake the formation turned South for Newcastle but it was too late; radar stations were tracking them and 13 Group's fighters were getting airborne. The enemy forces suffered grievous losses. Seven Me110s and eight Heinkel 111s were shot down. The Me110 leader, with a signals specialist and his equipment in the back seat, was blown to pieces when his long range belly fuel tank was hit. The formations scattered and headed for home. No. 12 Group thought the raiders might move South, so sent fighters up. In fact, the bombers that came in were 50 unescorted Ju88s of KG30 from Denmark. They headed for Driffield where they destroyed 10 Whitleys on the ground; the formation lost seven of its number.

The Luftwaffe had tried its flanking attack and had found the defences well prepared. Its losses were such that August 15th proved to be the first and last mass daylight raid on the North East. Luftflotte 5's units were gradually transferred to the Southern battleground. The system had more than proved its worth.

You may well ask why the Luftwaffe took so long to unravel the British system and to appreciate its strength. First, Luftwaffe air intelligence was the responsibility of a convivial, but exceedingly stupid, Colonel named Beppo Schmidt. To our great good fortune nearly all his major assumptions regarding the Royal Air Force, its organisation and equipment proved wrong. He did not understand technicalities, least of all radar and fighter control. They hardly figured in his reports.

Second, the Luftwaffe was dedicated to offence. Having steam-rollered its way across Scandinavia and Western Europe, everyone from Goering downwards gave scant thought to defending the Fatherland. The idea seemed vaguely ludicrous and even defeatist.

Third, the Luftwaffe did not have the remarkable integration of scientists and service personnel achieved by the RAF. They worked as one. Also, Hitler – a dictator — banned radio hams while we, in a democracy, had thousands of them; they knew all about valves and circuits and much more besides. These people were absorbed into the RAF and proved indispensable in radio, radar and a variety of other aids.

The Battle of Britain showed that a sophisticated air defence system actually existed – and that it worked. Even then, it took some time for the Luftwaffe to react on its home ground. It was not until well into 1941 that it began to assemble the basic assets. In the meantime, the RAF had learned a lot, extended its operational research and had introduced GCI radars for interception.

Anti Aircraft Defences of the North

Chairman:

No account of the Defence of Northern Skies would be complete without proper reference to the contribution made by the Anti Aircraft Regiments and Batteries of the Royal Artillery. The story of the development of AA defences and their integration with the Dowding System is a fascinating one in which many of the problems of later years in the SAM age were tackled and often solved.

Philip ANNIS was a National Service Gunner whose professional career was as a Curator. He was Deputy Director of the National Maritime Museum before retiring to join the Royal Artillery Institution as Editor of the Regimental History series. He has prepared a paper which sheds great light on the problems of AA defence, and the achievements of the RA in the North.

For almost all practical purposes, apart from a small number of guns sent at Churchill's request, as First Lord of the Admiralty, to the Humber, the Tyne, Rosyth and Invergordon, there was no AA defence of North-East England and eastern and northern Scotland during the First World War. Anti-aircraft defences were allotted to London and the South-East of England and to the field armies in Europe and the Near and Middle East.

The First World War saw not only the birth of anti-aircraft artillery in this country but also the development of the scientific study of the problems of engaging a target which moved at high speed in three dimensions in space. This study came to fruition in the middle 1920s as the Textbook of Anti-Aircraft Gunnery. It produced also a statement of the purpose of this new form of defence:

"The true criterion of the efficiency of the AA defence guns is not the number of aircraft destroyed, but rather what more the enemy could have accomplished in the absence of the AA artillery."

At the same time the important lesson drawn from the First World War was the need to integrate air and anti-aircraft activities. This had been done in home defence by General Ashmore on the basis of the separate zoning of guns and aircraft avoiding the indiscriminate mixture of these that had obtained earlier. The London Air Defence Area of 1918 was the result and Ashmore's concepts were followed in the Second World War at home and abroad. Thinking further ahead the Steel-Bartholemew plan (1923) and the discussion which followed led, in part, to the creation of a new command of the Royal Air Force, Air Defence of Great Britain (ADGB). Although the War Office was responsible for command, armament, recruitment and training, the anti-aircraft element of five gun brigades (regiments) of the Royal Artillery and five searchlight groups (battalions) of the Royal Engineers were placed under the operational command of ADGB. Although changes of title would happen in the future to both air and land elements the air would always retain operational control, first at home and later overseas though the arrangement did not always obtain in some theatres for local reasons.

An ADGB plan was drawn up, extended, extended again through the 1930s. New aircraft and new guns began to appear and greater attention was paid to other parts of the country; original planning having been largely concerned with London and the south-east of England.

There was recognition of the fact that centres of population, ports and naval bases, airfields, factories and means of communication would all require defence against air attack and further recognition that neither the Royal Air Force nor the Royal Artillery possessed the resources to meet the requirement. One result of this was the order, in 1938, that the Territorial Army should be doubled in size. A major part of the TA was engaged in AA duty one way or another. The AA defence of the UK would depend on Territorials. Regular AA units were earmarked for service overseas and some were serving there already when the war began.

When the RAF established its experimental radar establishment at Bawdsey an Army cell was added to it. The RAF was primarily concerned with distant early warning and this led to Chain Home. The Army cell wanted local early warning, at first to aid the existing visual instruments, but in due course wanted to add to it a means of directing fire accurately when the enemy came within range and a first model of a radar set for heavy anti-aircraft (HAA) artillery was made at Bawdsey. It became the prototype for sets to be built by commercial firms. The set would become known as the gun laying radar AA Mark I, or GL I. This was an inaccurate term in that it could not, on its own, provide the information required to lay a gun as it offered no information about the height of a target. Some of the sets were intermingled with Chain Home stations and, provided they were positioned high up, on cliff tops or purpose built towers, were valuable for the location of low flying aircraft which were reported directly to sector filter rooms. The two important guns of the period were the Vickers 3.7-inch HAA gun and the Bofors 40mm LAA gun. The 3-inch 20cwt high angle gun developed by the Royal Navy and introduced in 1913 was in service in far greater numbers even though its performance was inferior to that of the 3.7-inch. Some 3-inch and all 3.7-inch guns had magslip connection to a predictor. Searchlights were the province of the Royal Engineers, and also under RAF operational control, but in 1939/40 the battalions concerned transformed themselves into regiments of the Royal Artillery. Sound locators were also employed to give warning of approach and in 1939 an instrument appeared, the Visual Indicating Equipment (VIE), which presented the sound received on a cathode-ray tube screen; this, of course, was not a form of radar nor was the reliance on slow moving sound that effective. Searchlight regiments had the additional task of plotting raid movements for sector operations rooms and used instruments similar to those employed by the Observer Corps. In essence all components within ADGB and then Fighter Command worked under unified command and control in action primarily using the regional operations rooms provided by RAF sectors.

Lieutenant General Sir Frederick Pile, in succession to Lieutenant General Alan Brooke, commanded the new AA Command throughout the war and his command suffered repeated depredation at the hands of the War Office; trained regiments were taken from him for service overseas almost as a matter of course yet the training of AA troops required much more than was needed elsewhere in the army. The basic problem lay in the fact that Pile needed a larger proportion of better educated men, after all AA Command was the most scientific part of the Army and it was its scientists who developed operational research for the service. He also required a lot of people as he had to cover the entire UK. He therefore recruited women from the ATS, setting up mixed-manned HAA and searchlight regiments and borrowed a fair part of the Home Guard first for his Z (rocket) batteries and later for other HAA duties.

The tremendous expansion of the Royal Regiment in 1939/40 and the consequent need for control of the huge increase in AA personnel led to the establishment of two AA corps made up of seven AA divisions, later growing to three corps and 12 divisions. In the period from the outbreak of war to February 1941 we are concerned with 3rd and 7th AA Divisions and, later, with 10th. Broadly speaking 3rd AA Division was responsible for Scotland apart from Glasgow and the South-West. Orkney and Shetland Defences (OSDEF) were under 3rd AA Division's control and responsible for the islands to the north especially the fleet anchorage at Scapa Flow. 7th AA Division was charged with the protection of Cumberland, Northumberland, Co Durham and a slice of the North Riding and 10th Division, when established, with the area covering York, Leeds, Sheffield, Doncaster and Grimsby. The main Gun Defended Areas were the Humber, the Tees and the Tyne, extensions north would soon be added especially to cover the Forth. It was this basic layout, a descendant of the Reorientation Scheme, that had to face the raids of General Stumpff's Luftflotte 5 and Field Marshal Kesselring's Luftflotte 2 in co-operation with the aircraft of No. 13 Group and part of No. 12 Group together with Nos. 33 and 34 Balloon Barrage Groups of the RAF.

Some idea of the strength allotted in September 1939 may be drawn from the following:

Divs	Bdes	HAA Regts	LAA Regts	SL Regts
3rd	36	71, 94, 101		
	42	74, 83, 100		
	52			51, 52, 56, 57
	51		14, 18, 19, 31, 32	
7th	30	63, 64, 87		37, 53
	31	66, 96		
	39	62, 67, 91		40, 46
	43	85		47, 54, 55
	57		13, 28, 29, 30	

This shows nine brigades containing 15 HAA, nine LAA and 11 searchlight (SL) regiments. All would have been understrength, engaged in recruitment and training and would be lacking most of their intended equipment; all were part of the Territorial Army. Equipment included, in heavy regiments, the 3-inch, converted to accept direction from a predictor, and the new 3.7-inch designed from the outset to use predicted data; in LAA hands there were so few 40mm guns that most regiments were armed with 0.303-inch machine guns and some had 20mm Hispanos though there were some Vickers 2-pounders on naval mountings and unconverted 3-inch guns fitted with deflector sights. The searchlight position was better and included new 90cm projectors while even newer 150cm projectors were coming forward; both would benefit from the fitting of searchlight control radar in due course.

The first raid of the war in which HAA guns were employed took place over the Forth in October 1939 where a gun site damaged a raider and a fighter then shot it down. On 7th March 1940 228th HAA Battery of 94th HAA Regiment was deployed in the defence of Aberdeen. RAF radar spotted an He111 and informed the guns. The gun position calculated the height of the target and passed the information to the RAF. The enemy aircraft then climbed until it was out of gun range. Fighters appeared and the guns fired salvoes at the target at fuse settings of 22, 28 and 30 seconds while the Spitfires continued to gain height. The He111 varied its height and each alteration was calculated by the guns and passed to the fighters which, guided by shell bursts, shot down the raider at 26,000 feet. This technique of the employment of 'pointer rounds', though not new, was further developed as time went on even though GCI and AI were brought into use. Similarly, searchlights were employed not only to illuminate a target at night but as guides to night fighters and as beacons for returning bombers as well as forming an important part of the raid information chain.

General Pile, at Stanmore, was charged with the allocation of guns and searchlights to particular areas subject to the overall direction of the AOC-in-C Fighter Command, Air Chief Marshal Sir Hugh Dowding (Fighter Command had to an extent succeeded ADGB in 1936), and inevitably the bulk was sent to South of the line from the Humber to the Severn with an extension to industrial South Wales. Guns and searchlights for eastern northern England and Scotland were primarily positioned round the ports and industrial cities as well as at Scapa Flow but there were continuous calls for more defences everywhere. The Forth and Rosyth, Invergordon, Dundee, Aberdeen, the Moray Firth were just a few of the places needing defences. Starting in January 1940 more 3.7 and naval 4.5-inch guns were allocated to 3rd AA Division but only ten extra 40mm were available to cope with low flying raiders. LAA defences, mostly machine guns, were provided for industrial and military sites and airfields. The raid on Scapa Flow on 16th March demonstrated that the area required to be covered by concentrations of fire was beyond the range of the guns which had to be sited round the edge of that huge expanse of water.

Matters improved slowly; from war diaries of the time it is clear that the introduction of more radar sets, the greater number of trained personnel and the more formally worked out division of responsibility for guns and fighters were mainly responsible for this. A feature of the raiding in 1939 and the first half of 1940 in the North-East was that it was carried out either by single aircraft or by small groups and mostly by He111s. The assumptions made by AA Gunners at the time were that the Germans were engaged in armed reconnaissance or operational training rather than in the more formal pattern of the much larger raids further South; Luftflotte 5 was indeed more concerned with reconnaissance, mining and attacks on shipping though would have its bomber element increased in due course. Raids were also very scattered. The Humber, the Tyne, the Forth, Dundee and Aberdeen were raided fairly regularly but by so few aircraft that it was hard to see their purpose other than that of reconnaissance and training. Damage was usually light and it appeared that standards of navigation and aim were low. Heavier raids were aimed at the industrial cities of the North and Midlands of England and at Glasgow and Belfast but even these were usually not of the same order of size as those further south.

Reporting procedures were vital. In essence, reports were passed to the filter room and then onto the sector operations room which contained not only the RAF controller but also the commander of the appropriate AA brigade acting as Anti-Aircraft Defence Commander (AADC). Searchlight batteries also reported to the filter room as did the Chain Home radar sites and the Observer Corps. The sector operations room, taking its information from the filter room, used its control links to issue instructions and information to airfields and gun and searchlight positions and at the same time kept group operations informed. There were AA liaison officers at sector and group levels and the AA division covering the area had its links with group operations as well as its brigades and regiments. The guns were controlled from a gun operations room (GOR), commanded by an AADC, in each Gun Defended Area at brigade or regimental level whichever was appropriate and it, the filter room, sector operations room and group operations room all worked off the same gridded map. The system worked well as Gunner liaison officers and RAF controllers worked side by side both upwards to group and brigade/division and downwards to fighters and guns. It had been developed from procedures first worked out at Uxbridge by No. 11 Group RAF and AA Command. The "Uxbridge" system formed the pattern for other groups in Fighter Command and was adopted by large area defences overseas in due course.

Guns, of course, could open fire on the initiative of local commanders down to the Gun Position Officer (the subaltern commanding two or four guns) but rules of engagement were very strict to minimise the chances of fire being opened on friendly or neutral aircraft. The basic test was that a gun site should recognise an enemy as hostile and often under difficult conditions of identification a hostile act had to be committed before the guns could open 'unseen' fire. Light anti-aircraft guns were usually forbidden to fire 'unseen' at night. Fire was checked if friendly aircraft were about. Frequently sector operations rooms ordered all guns to cease fire if there was the possibility, however remote, that friendly aircraft might be endangered. Sector operations rooms, in the early years of the war, often faced considerable problems in tracking and identifying fighters at night.

The technique of engaging 'unseen' targets, at night or in very cloudy conditions, was in its infancy. If there were no friendly fighters about then the VIE associated with the sound locators would give a very general idea of an enemy aircraft's position but the only means of engaging it was the expensive one of firing concentrations, known then and ever afterwards by the erroneous title 'barrages'.

The organisation still left something to be desired but through 1940 and 1941 and into 1942 the pressure of events militated against much in the way of change. Weapons were manufactured in larger numbers and a new radar, the GLII came into service enabling unseen targets to be engaged by predicted fire as predictors were amended to accept radar data. The same year also saw the introduction of the 3-inch (Z) rocket. Large numbers could be launched at once and had a marked deterrent effect against raiders as the usual fire unit consisted of 64 twin launchers, the rockets had a similar lethality to, though lacked the range of, the 3.7-inch gun and early allocations were made to the large Gun Defended Areas on the coast, Hull being one of the first. The middle of 1942 saw Z regiments defending Durham and Edinburgh with a detached battery at Thurso. More 40mm Bofors arrived but recourse was still had to 3-inch guns and machine guns in many places.

The Battle of Britain and the night 'Blitz' drew regiments South, in part uncovering or thinning the defences of the area with which we are concerned. Nevertheless aircraft and guns defended the British left flank to such an extent that little damage was done. The achievements of Nos. 12 and 13 Groups and 7th AA Division on 15th August 1940 in driving off attacks against the Tyne and the Humber were outstanding.

The greater number of night fighters with AI radar was beginning to play its part as well though ironically, when the RAF ordered 'Fighter Nights', AA Command was subject to bitter criticism from the public who had come to rely on the 'comforting' sound of the guns taking the war to the enemy; the larger picture was not easy to follow for those not immediately involved in its painting.

The order of battle for AA Command in February 1941 in the north and east included:

2nd AA Corps

Div	Bdes	HAA Regts	LAA Regts	SL Regts	Area
10th	31		38, 71	43, 49, 54	W. Yorks
	39	62, 91	39	30, 40, 84	Humber, Scunthorpe
	62	75, 96, 117	59		Leeds, Sheffield

A total of five HAA, four LAA and six SL regiments.

3rd AA Corps

Divs	Bdes	HAA Regts	LAA Regts	SL Regts	Area
3rd	36	71, 114	31, 32		Edinburgh, Forth
	51	108	40, 67		NE Scotland
	52			51, 52, 56	RAF Sectors
7th	30	63, 64	37, 68		Tyne
	43	8, 73	50, 72	47, 55	Tees, Middlesbrough
	57			46, 53	RAF Sectors

A total of seven HAA, eight LAA and seven SL regiments.

AA Command

OSDEF	HAA Regts	LAA Regts	SL Regts
	65, 66, 81	19	38*, 39, 59

A total of three HAA, one LAA and the best part of three SL regiments *38 SL being incomplete.

Night attacks during the winter of 1940-41 were made on Hull and Sheffield and in 1942 on Hull, Middlesbrough and York. In 1943 Hull was attacked quite frequently by night. Aberdeen, Newcastle, Sunderland and Grimsby were also important targets and some of the raids were far heavier than before with 60 plus aircraft attacking Hull on 13th July followed by 50 plus twelve days later. In the 'Baby Blitz' of the first half of 1944 Hull was attacked twice; by 131 aircraft on 19th March and by 130 on 12th April.

In 1942 AA Command reorganised from corps and divisions into groups of which there were seven, each group containing a number of AA brigades. With its HQ in Edinburgh 6th AA Group was responsible for the whole of Scotland and 5th Group, HQ in Nottingham, took over the eastern side of England as far south as Norfolk. OSDEF, with two AA brigades, now came directly under AA Command. These groups closely matched the geographical areas covered by Fighter Command's own groups.

The middle years of the war saw changes in raiding patterns. This was the period of 'Fringe Targets' ('tip-and-run raids') and 'Baedeker Raids'. The former involved the South of England only but the latter applied to our area. York was an early victim as was Edinburgh. Middlesbrough was attacked at the same time. Again the attacks were usually half-hearted but occasionally heavy and Luftflotte 2 was involved in them more than the smaller Luftflotte 5 in Norway. What was required to meet these raids was more 40mm guns but the demands for these elsewhere, not least from the field armies overseas, naval bases, the Desert Air Force and the large number of airfields in North-East India as well as the 'Baedeker' towns of the South and West of England, meant that as always numbers for the North-East were reduced as units were sent to more threatened areas. In the Autumn of 1942 the defences with which we are concerned were provided by AA brigades with their HQs at Kirkwall, Hoy, Inverness, Aberdeen, South Queensferry, Gosforth, Gateshead and Stockton-on-Tees.

A development of the period was the introduction of Chain Home Low (CHL) and, later, the centrimetric Chain Home Extra Low

(CHEL) to give earlier warning of low level approach. CHL was originally closely related to Coast Defence radar though became entirely a matter for the RAF; the co-location of the services at Bawdsey produced many valuable spin-offs and included the adoption of naval radar by the Army and the RAF. Coast Defence radar, of course, played its part in the raid reporting chain. Then came the appearance of a new radar, the American SCR 584, known to the British as Radar No. 3 Mark V, and the American Bell AAA Predictor, known in this country as Predictor No. 10. Heavy anti-aircraft shooting performance improved with this introduction of automatic tracking radar and electronic computing in prediction which together resulted in the semi-automatic control of fire instead of the old and tortuous manual process. To these must be added the VT or radio proximity fuse. This combination of radar, predictor and fuse played a major part in defeating the V1.

In 1944 AA Command was faced with further tasks, the protection of 21st Army Group during its preparation for 'Overlord' and the onset of 'Diver' the V1 counter-offensive. Again resources were taken from northern England and Scotland, only Scapa Flow being untouched. HQ 6th AA Group was transferred to Portsmouth, leaving only sketchy defences. Operation 'Diver' also concerns us in that V1s launched from Holland or from He111s over the North Sea did present a threat to North-East England. 'Diver' defences were extended to the 'Fringe' area stretching from Skegness to Bridlington, incorporating the existing Gun Defended Area of the Humber, and were further increased to north of Filey. All these defences were in the hands of 5th AA Group. 'Diver' deployments were specially designed to match the characteristics of their targets. The V1 threat to northern skies was never very great so it is understandable that defences to counter it were sketchy. In spite of these lasting heavy commitments, AA Command continued to be ordered to give up units for employment elsewhere. It was worth remembering that, in co-operation with United States Artillery, gunner regiments, some of them 'mixed' (ie containing a large number of women) played an important role in the defence of Antwerp and Brussels against extensive V1 attacks.

As the measure of the V1 was being taken planning ensued for the further defence of the North and North-East. 5th AA Group would be responsible for Tees, Tyne and Humber and 8th for the Forth and Clyde. OSDEF continued as before still with a sizeable number of regiments.

The end of the war led to an examination of everything to do with anti-aircraft artillery. The plan of 1947 envisaged that 3rd AA Group would afford defence to Forth and Clyde and 5th AA Group would be charged with Tyne, Tees, industrial South Yorkshire and the Midlands. 3rd AA Group would consist of one Regular and four Territorial AA brigades while 5th would have four Regular and nine Territorial AA brigades.

The post war requirement for economy led to a continuing search for reductions in the cost of the armed forces. Modernisation plans for AA gradually fell by the wayside. An improved 40mm made its appearance, indeed the Bofors is still going strong today though not in this country. Attempts were made to produce a new HAA gun but the project demonstrated that a gun capable of dealing with fast jet bombers flying at great height would be very large and very expensive. Further, the threat from high flying jet bombers was aggravated by the possibility of nuclear attack. The counter to this could best be provided by jet fighters and high speed guided missiles. Other projects, some of them very promising in the medium range up to 25,000 feet, were started but did not come into service. New radars did appear with greater range and the use of a diversity of frequencies. By 1954 it was concluded that the 1947 plan could not be met and AA Command was abolished in 1955.

Air defence was now firmly in the hands of aircraft though short-range guided weapons, both hand-held and vehicle-mounted, appeared for use by the Royal Artillery for the defence of forces in the field. One long-range mobile guided weapon, 'Thunderbird', appeared which deployed for a time in the hands of the Royal Artillery in Germany but changes in defence policy led to its abandonment. The same changes led also to the end of the Regiment's part in the defence of northern skies.

This paper presents simply an overview. The constraints of space mean that much relevant information has had to be omitted. The following works are of great importance in understanding what was done in the anti-aircraft field and why:

1. *Anti-Aircraft Artillery 1914-55*, by Brigadier N. W. Routledge, Brassey's (UK), London, 1994, the fourth volume in the New Series of the *History of the Royal Regiment of Artillery*. Brigadier Routledge also contributed the anti-aircraft chapter to the third volume in the series *Between the Wars 1919-39* (Brassey's 1992). Practically all of this paper is based on Norman Routledge's work which is a most valuable corrective to a great deal of what has been written in the past

and is essential reading for students of the history of air warfare.

2. *Text Book of Anti-Aircraft Gunnery,* Two volumes, HMSO, London, 1924/5.

3. *Ack-Ack,* by General Sir Frederick Pile, George G. Harrap & Co. Ltd., London, 1949.

4. *Army Radar,* by Brigadier A. P. Sayer, War Office, London 1950.

5. *The Defence of the United Kingdom,* by Basil Collier, HMSO, London, 1957

Sound Mirror at Fulwell near Sunderland shown in 1995
(Kevin Brady)

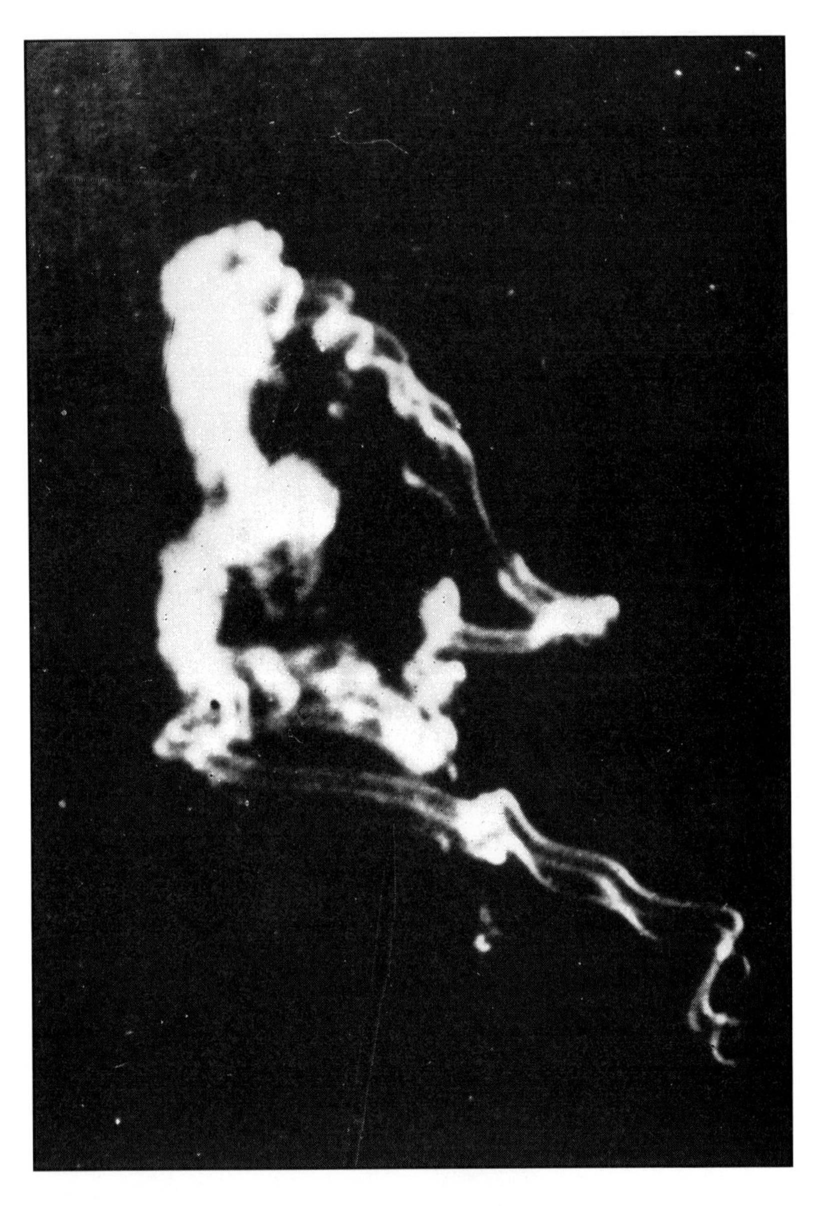

The last moments of Zeppelin L.34, captured by an amateur photographer. The airship was shot down over Hartlepool Bay by 2nd Lt. I.V. Pyott of No. 36 Squadron RFC from Seaton Carew. Kapitänleutnant Max Dietrich and his crew of 19 were killed.
(Robert Jackson)

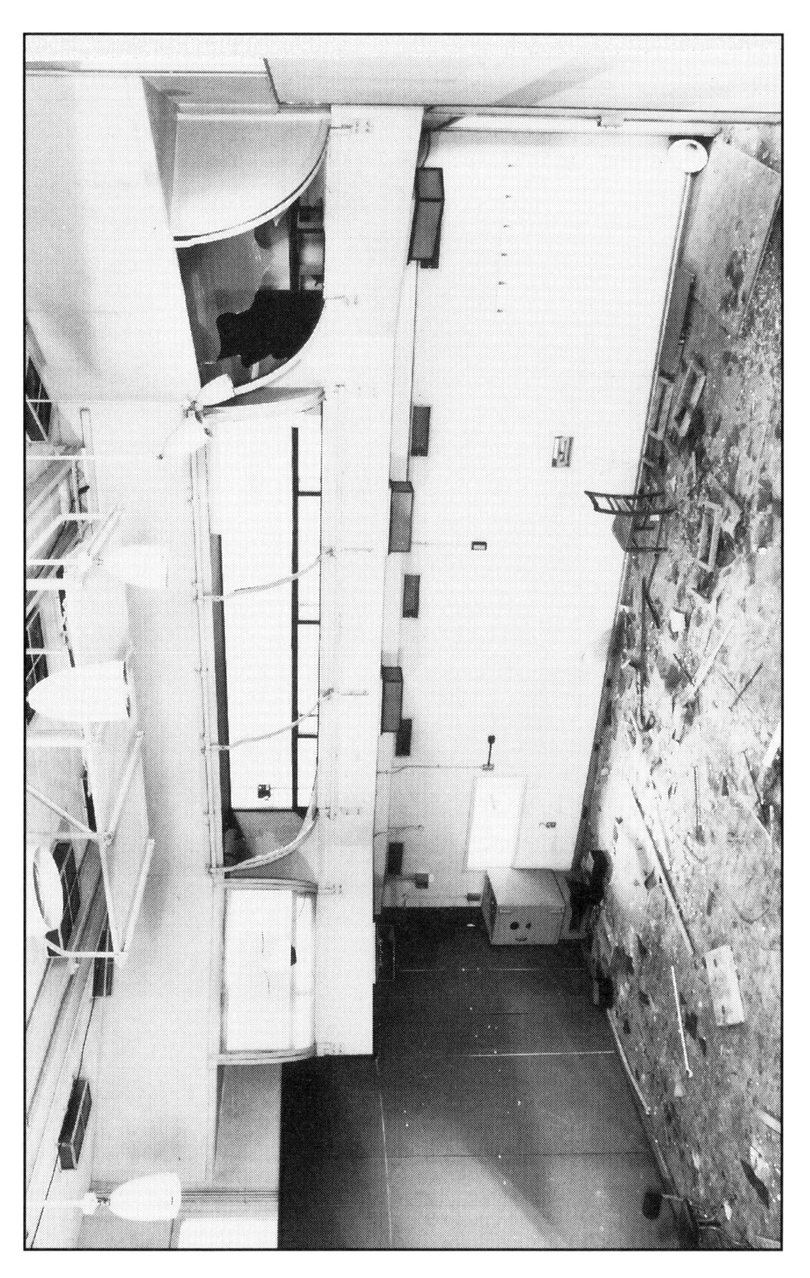

Operations Room of No. 13 Group shown 55 years after the Battle of Britain
(Roger Thomas RCHME ©Crown Copyright)

Spitfires of No. 72 Sqn over Holy Island Sands
(Robert Jackson)

Receiver of GL Mk II gunnery fire control radar used with HAA Batteries
(RA Historical Trust via Philip Annis)

Beaufighter VI KV 975 of C Sqn., 54 OTU, Winfield 1944
flown by Flt Lt Don Steele RCAF on 21 Nov. 44
(via Historical Radar Archive)

Mosquito Night Fighter of No. 409 Sqn, RCAF

—	—	—	—	—	—	—						
						TOTALS BROUGHT FORWARD	37:20	80:10			98:05	470:45
NOV	6	BEAU VI	109	SELF	CPL. GILBERT	a/c TEST						:20
		"	239	"		a/c & WEATHER TEST						:45
	7	"	230	"	F/L PHILLIPS	TO NORTHSTEAD & RETURN WEATHER U/S						:10
		"	233	"	SGT DEVON	a/c TEST						:35
	9	"	8620	"	F/L KNOWLES N/R, P/O MOULD, F/O PAGE	NAVIGATOR'S CHECK						:45
	11	"	109	"	F/O MILES, SGT. REES	NAVIGATOR'S CHECK						:30
		"	"	"	P/O DENNIS, SGT. WEBB, W/O HOGG	NAVIGATOR'S CHECK						:40
		"	"	"	P/O WIGMORE, SGT. WADDELL	NAVIGATOR'S CHECK						:30
	13	"	109	"	SGT MARTIN, P/O STUART, P/O RAYNER, W/O HOGG	NAVIGATORS' CHECKS						:35
	18	"	919	"	P/O PENTON	TO ACKLINGTON						:25
		"	"	"	"	ENGINE TEST & TO BASE						1:45
	20	"	231	"		WINFIELD TO CHARTER HALL						:25
		"	269	F/L MCKWAN	SELF	TO WINFIELD						
	21	"	975	SELF	W/O LOMAN, P/O ZOWSKY, SGT EMMERSON	1ST DEMO "C" SQDN						1:40
		"	850	"	F/L TOPHAM, F/O ZOWSKY, P/O DASH	1ST DEMO						:55
	22	"	214	"		AIR TEST						:10
	25	"	975	"	F/L STONEBRIDGE, P/O BROWN, F/O CHRISTIE	EX L						1:15
		"	219	"		TARGET						:55
	29	"	883	"	SGT MORRELL, SGT SCOTT, F/O WINGHAM	WINDOW EX.						2:00
	30	"	271	"	P/O DASH, P/O ANDREWS'S, W/O MCDONOUGH	WINDOW PORT ENG U/S S.E. LDG.						:45
		"	199	"		a/c TEST						:30
			S/L	SUMMARY FOR NOV 1944		1. BEAU VI						19:15
				UNIT 54 O.T.U.	"B" & "C" SQDN	2.						
				DATE 1/12/44		3.						
				SIGNATURE Don J Steele								
				GRAND TOTAL [Cols. (1) to (10)] 943 Hrs. 00 Mins.		TOTALS CARRIED FORWARD	37:20	30:10			98:05	486:20

O.C. "C" FLIGHT [signature]

Page from log book of Flt Lt Don Steele
(Mrs Sarah Steele)

Type 7 GCI radar. Operational at Northstead, Northumberland on 10 Aug. 43
(via Historical Radar Archive)

Meteor F8s of No. 43 Sqn,

Defence against the Intruders - 1940-45

Chairman:

Much has been written about the air defence of the British Isles, especially about the Battle of Britain, but little about events in the North. Robert JACKSON turns the spotlight on a little known aspect of the air defence of Northern Skies, the intruder raids which were so damaging to morale yet were countered effectively in due course of time.

In mid-May 1940, in the wake of the German Blitzkrieg in France and the Low Countries, Royal Air Force Bomber Command began operations for the first time against oil and communications targets in Germany, having hitherto confined itself to fringe attacks directed mainly against naval facilities. Such raids, mounted in growing strength, were intolerable to the Nazi leadership and in particular to Reichsmarschall Hermann Goering, the Luftwaffe C-in-C, who had earlier boasted that if enemy bombs ever fell on the Reich territory people might call him Meier - a predominantly Jewish name.

It is untrue that the Luftwaffe's pre-war planners had given no thought to the night defence of Germany. Even before the war, an Me 109 squadron at Greifswald was assigned to night-fighting practice with the aid of searchlights, and a specialist night-fighter unit, 10/JG

26, also equipped with Me 109s, was on the order of battle in September 1939, although it was very much experimental.

The unsuitability of the Me 109 for night-fighter operations quickly became apparent, and following the start of the RAF's strategic offensive the first effective night-fighter units were formed, equipped in the main with Me 110s. In addition to these, a specialist long-range night-fighter unit, I/NJG 2, was also established with three squadrons of Junkers 88s and one of Dornier 17s. Tasked with long-range night-fighter operations, this was the Luftwaffe's first night intruder Gruppe, and early in August 1940 it deployed forward to Gilze-Rijn in Holland, from where it began operations against the British Isles in September under the command of Hauptmann Karl-Heinrich Heyse.

The Gruppe's operational area over Britain was divided into three sectors. Sector One covered an area bounded by the Thames estuary, northern London, the East Midlands and the Wash, taking the whole of East Anglia; Sector Two ran inland from the Wash to Birmingham, then swung North to Sheffield and North-East to the Humber, covering Lincolnshire and South Yorkshire; while Sector Three, which is of relevance to our theme, ran from the Humber to Sheffield, Sheffield-Leeds, Leeds-Blackpool and finally from Blackpool to a point on the Northumbrian coast north of Newcastle upon Tyne. This was the only sector to extend as far as the West coast and was the largest in area – although by no means the most important, as the other two encompassed the two areas where Bomber Command had its densest concentration of airfields.

After some preliminary sorties over Lincolnshire in late August and September 1940, the intruders brought their war to the Northernmost sector on 21 September, when Hauptmann Karl Hülshoff destroyed a Whitley of No 58 Squadron, the aircraft crashing near Thornaby with the loss of all four crew. Three nights later, Feldwebel Hans Hahn shot down a 102 Squadron Whitley near Linton-on-Ouse. In the early hours of 28 September Lindholme was attacked by Leutnant Heinz Völker, who damaged a Hampden of 49 Squadron as it was landing and shot down a second just off the coast.

During this initial period of operations the intruders lost four aircraft, although only one is thought to have been destroyed by the air defences - in this instance by anti-aircraft fire. During October and November the sortie rate was low, but in December several sorties were flown against the Lincolnshire airfields, in the course of which a Dornier 17 was destroyed and another damaged by Hurricanes of No 12 Group flying night patrols. During one of these sorties, the Gruppe commander, Major Karl-Heinrich Heyse, was shot down and killed by the Manby airfield defences.

Meanwhile, Fighter Command had been compelled to adopt what might best be described as desperation measures to counter the enemy night raiders, for the Luftwaffe's main force night offensive against Britain was now in full swing. Six squadrons of Bristol Blenheims, converted to carry airborne radar, did not provide a solution to the night defence problem; they were too slow, the equipment was very unreliable, and its operators lacked experience. A solution was on the horizon in the shape of the fast, heavily armed Bristol Beaufighter, which was just entering service; but this aircraft was beset by more than the usual crop of teething troubles. In November and December 1940, Beaufighters and radar-equipped Blenheims flew over 600 sorties, made 71 radar contacts, and succeeded in destroying only four enemy aircraft.

In September 1940, Air Chief Marshal Sir Hugh Dowding, the AOC-in-C Fighter Command, had been ordered by the Air Council to allocate three squadrons of Hawker Hurricanes to night defence, this decision having been taken following the creation of a high-level Night Air Defence Committee earlier in the month. Added to these were three squadrons of Boulton-Paul Defiants, aircraft which, armed solely with a four-gun power-operated turret, had suffered appalling losses in the day fighter role during the Battle of Britain. During the closing weeks of 1940, these six squadrons of single-engined fighters flew 491 sorties on 46 nights and destroyed eleven enemy bombers.

In December 1940 No 4 Operational Training Unit - later renamed No 54 OTU - was established at Church Fenton to train night-fighter crews. It may be that Luftwaffe Intelligence got wind of the OTU's activities, because on the night of 15 January 1941 the station was attacked by an intruding Junkers 88 of NJG2, which badly damaged two Defiants and a Blenheim. Earlier in the month, another intruder had also attacked and badly damaged a No 10 Squadron Whitley near Catterick.

On the night of 10 February 1941 the intruders threw their weight against the Lincolnshire airfields of No 5 Group, destroying seven aircraft returning from raids on Germany and Holland. Despite encounters with RAF night-fighters, all the intruders - nine aircraft - returned to base.

Since November 1940, No 600 Squadron, which had brought its Blenheim night-fighters north to Catterick in the previous month, had been in the process of conversion to Beaufighters; it was declared operational in March 1941, when it moved to Drem for a fortnight before departing for Colerne in Wiltshire. Another Beaufighter squadron, No 68, also formed at Catterick early in the year, but in April it was assigned to the defence of the Midlands.

Delays in the production of AI Mk IV airborne radar meant that the planned target of five Beaufighter squadrons would not be reached before the spring of 1941, and in the meantime it was the Blenheims, Defiants and Hurricanes that continued to hold the line. In the North, one Defiant squadron, No 141, was based at Ayr from the end of April 1941, and - with detachments at Acklington - found itself in the middle of the May 'Blitz' on Clydeside and Tyneside, its crews claiming eight victories. Although still not radar-equipped, the Defiant was proving itself unexpectedly suited to the night-fighter role; experience had taught crews that if the pilot could manoeuvre his aircraft to a position beneath an enemy bomber, the gunner, elevating his guns at an angle, could usually inflict punishing damage on it. It was a technique developed further by the Luftwaffe's night-fighter force later in the war, when aircraft fitted with fixed upwards-firing guns inflicted severe losses on the RAF's heavy bombers.

March 1941 was a significant month, for it saw the operational debut of Ground Controlled Interception (GCI) stations such as that at Patrington, on the Humber estuary. This, together with the conversion of five of Fighter Command's six Blenheim squadrons to Beaufighters, brought about a dramatic change in the Command's fortunes just in time to counter the Luftwaffe's 'Blitz' on London, Merseyside, Tyneside, Clydeside and other targets. The Hurricane and Defiant squadrons allocated to night defence also added to this change as a result of their increased experience, and because they too derived assistance from GCI. Hitherto, Sector Controllers had been able to bring night-fighter crews to within about five miles of a target, and since the range of AI Mk IV was only about three miles, it still needed a fair slice of luck to make a successful interception. The much more precise information provided by the GCI stations made the task far easier, and matters improved still further with the introduction of AI Mk VII, which had a seven-mile range and a low-level capability. For the first time, the MK VII, together with information passed on by the Chain Home Low radar stations - the low-level part of the general warning system - gave night-fighter crews the ability to intercept low-flying minelayers and reconnaissance aircraft which had been operating off the North-East coast almost with impunity.

The figures themselves - and these are nationwide - speak for the general improvement in the overall air defence system by the summer of 1941. In February the enemy lost only four aircraft to fighters and eight to anti-aircraft, but during March night-fighters shot down 22 enemy bombers and the AA guns seventeen. In April the score rose to 48 for the fighters and 39 for the guns, and in the first two weeks of May the loss rate assumed serious proportions, 96 bombers being shot down by fighters and 32 by AA guns. In addition, ten others were lost due to unknown causes.

Following a final spate of intense attacks on London, the Midlands and Merseyside, the Luftwaffe's spring 'Blitz' on Britain gradually petered out at the end of May 1941 as the Germans transferred the bulk of their bomber force to the east in readiness for Operation Barbarossa, the invasion of Russia, or to the Balkans. Although bombing attacks on the North continued on a sporadic basis during 1941, these tended to follow intruder-type tactics, only small numbers of aircraft being involved.

As for the dedicated intruder squadrons, these continued to concentrate on the bomber bases of Lincolnshire and East Anglia in the spring of 1941, and forays into northern airspace were few. Nevertheless, they did occur, and on the night of 16/17 April a Ju 88 flown by Feldwebel Wilhelm Breetz, one of NJG 2's most experienced pilots, fell victim to the Tyne anti-aircraft defences. (The 7th Anti-Aircraft Division, incidentally, was responsible for defending the region, covering Tees-side and Tyneside.) Another experienced intruder pilot, Leutnant Heinz Völker, had better luck in the early hours of 26 April, destroying a Blenheim and a Defiant at Church Fenton and damaging two more aircraft in a combined bombing and strafing attack. Völker also claimed two more aircraft destroyed that night in attacks on the Lincolnshire airfields.

Intruder attacks continued during June and were again directed against Lincolnshire and East Anglia, but on the night of the 13th the intruders suffered a severe set back when three Junkers 88s failed to return, all falling victim to the Beaufighters of No 25 Squadron from Wittering. This was not, however, by any means the beginning of the end for the intruders. Beaufighters accounted for only three more before the middle of October, although others fell to anti-aircraft fire and, in one case, to a Douglas Havoc night-fighter of No 85 Squadron. More of the Havoc later.

What did spell the end of intruder operations over England was a personal instruction from Adolf Hitler on 13 October 1941, ordering them to cease. The reason was purely one of propaganda. With the RAF's night-bombing effort steadily increasing, Hitler wanted the German people to see the 'terror bombers' destroyed over the Reich territory; far-away victories over England did nothing to improve their morale. For General Kammhuber, commanding Germany's night defences, it was a bitter blow; what was potentially his most potent weapon had been struck from his hand, and no argument would sway the Fuhrer.

What, then, had the intruder force - which never numbered more than twenty or thirty serviceable aircraft - achieved in just over a year of operations? It had certainly destroyed over 50 aircraft over England, together with an estimated 30 more over the North Sea. About 40 others sustained damage as a consequence of intruder attacks. The cost to the Germans was 27 aircraft, plus seven more destroyed in accidents.

After many pitfalls, as we have seen, the RAF's night-fighter defences were at last becoming organised. May 10th, 1941, had seen the formation of a night-fighter squadron which was to have a long-standing association with the North; this was No 406 Squadron, Royal Canadian Air Force, which formed at Acklington with Merlin-engined Beaufighters Mk II and scored its first success over Newcastle on 1 September. By the end of the year its score had risen to five destroyed and four damaged. Early in 1942 it moved to Drem, where it operated alongside a second RCAF night-fighter squadron, No 410, both squadrons detaching flights to various locations around the North. Four aircraft of No 406 were sent to Scorton, near Richmond in Yorkshire, in February 1942, and were joined later by the rest of the squadron.

In April 1942, the night air defence of the North rested on two squadrons of Beaufighters - 141 and 406 - and No 410, still equipped with Defiants and based at Drem. No 141 Squadron was at Acklington, which it shared with No 1460 Flight - an unhappy combination of No 43 Squadron Hurricanes and searchlight-equipped Havocs, which were supposed to detect and then illuminate the target for the accompanying single-engined fighter. No 1460 Flight, later renumbered 539 Squadron, was one of ten Turbinlite flights operating around the country. They were a complete waste of resources; although they claimed several interceptions and one or two enemy aircraft damaged before their disbandment early in 1943, they only succeeded in shooting one aircraft down, and that was a Stirling of 218 Squadron. Luckily, all the crew got out.

In other areas, however, thanks to improved GCI techniques and better radar, the night defences enjoyed more success. During the so-called Baedecker raids of 1942, when the Luftwaffe attacked targets of historic or cultural importance, night-fighters accounted for most of the 67 enemy bombers destroyed, mostly Dornier 217s of KG 2, between April and July.

I must make brief mention here of deception techniques, which contributed in no small measure to thwarting the enemy night offensive. By the end of 1941, airfields in the north and elsewhere were backed up by decoys known as 'Q' sites, with dummy flarepath and perimeter lighting laid out to resemble the pattern of the real aerodrome. According to some estimates, these decoy sites received seven times the number of bombs as those that fell on the real airfields. Most were closed down in the summer of 1944, when the bombing threat had receded.

Radio deception equipment was also installed; this included masking beacons, devised by the Radio Branch of the Post Office Engineering Department and designed to interfere with the Luftwaffe's radio navigational aids. Three such beacons, known as Meacons, were situated in the North, at Marske near Redcar, Reston near Eyemouth and Mintlaw near Peterhead. They achieved considerable success. On the night of 6/7th July 1941, for example, thanks to the jamming of the Noordwijk beacon, three Junkers 88s of Kustenfliegergruppe 106 operating between Holy Island and Whitby became disorientated and all three flew into high ground near Bridlington.

The year 1942 saw the debut of the night-fighter that really tipped the scales: the de Havilland Mosquito. In October No 25 Squadron became the North's first Mosquito night-fighter squadron, moving to Church Fenton and displacing No 54 OTU, which went to Charterhall on the Scottish Borders. Later in the month No 410 Squadron also re-equipped at Acklington.

The advent of the Mosquito was timely, for KG 2's fast Dorniers, which were capable of 300 mph at low altitude, were causing problems for the defences. And it was not only historic towns that were hit; Middlesbrough, for example, after a break of five months, was attacked four times between the middle of April and the end of July 1942. It is also worth recording that, outside the great conurbations of London and Merseyside, the hardest-hit city in Britain was Hull. By the war's end, only 6,000 out of 93,000 buildings in Hull had escaped bomb damage, most of it incurred during three major attacks in March and May 1941. Because of its geographical location, Hull was an easy target. It was heavily attacked twice during Operation Steinbock, the so-called 'Little Blitz' of January to May 1944, conducted by all available German bombers on the Western Front. During these two attacks, carried out by Junkers 88s, Dornier 217s and Heinkel 177s, No 25 Squadron (Coltishall), 264 Squadron (Church Fenton) and 307 Polish Squadron (Drem) claimed eleven enemy aircraft between them. As a matter of note, the 'Little Blitz' cost the Luftwaffe 329 aircraft, of which 129 were destroyed by Mosquitoes equipped with Mk VIII AI radar.

In 1943-44 the Luftwaffe once again mounted frequent intruder operations, using mainly Me 410 and Ju 188 aircraft. We can see a measure of what they might have achieved, had these aircraft been committed in greater numbers, in one attack on American air bases in East Norfolk on 2 April 1944, when intruders destroyed thirteen B-24 Liberators and, in the panic, two more were shot down by their own airfield defences. The Germans lost a single Me 410.

By the beginning of 1944, further improvements in the British air defences had made it hard for the Luftwaffe to penetrate into UK air space at medium and low level. Increased numbers of anti-aircraft guns of all calibres, rocket batteries capable of firing salvoes of 128 missiles, and radar-directed searchlights able to illuminate targets up to 35,000 feet all contributed to frustrating the attackers, and the fast enemy bombers now began to penetrate at up to 30,000 feet before diving on their objectives and making a high-speed exit. These new tactics caused problems for the night-fighters, since following an enemy aircraft in a dive meant that radar contact was often lost because of ground returns. The answer was to extend the night-fighter patrol lines well out to sea; many intruders were trapped and destroyed in this way, as indeed were many Heinkel 111s engaged in air-launching V-1 flying bombs in the closing weeks of the year. One of these missiles, launched at Manchester but badly off course, gave the people of the Durham village of Tudhoe a nasty shock when it blew up next door on Christmas Eve, 1944.

Had the Luftwaffe been in a position to launch a renewed night offensive against the North in the early summer of 1944, it would not have been left entirely to the RAF to counter the threat. By this time, radar-equipped Fairey Fireflies of No 784 Squadron, Fleet Air Arm, were operating from Drem as part of the integrated air defence system. It is interesting to note that the Navy's Fireflies did in fact operate against night intruders - but that was in Korea, in 1951, when several aircraft were deployed to Kimpo to form a defence flight against Po-2 biplanes making night attacks on United Nations forces. No claims were made.

At Scorton, the 422nd and 425th Squadrons of the US IXth Army Air Force, which had been training there for some weeks, were declared combat-ready early in June 1944. Equipped originally with Beaufighters, these squadrons now had a full complement of Northrop P-61 Black Widow night-fighters, and were also integrated with the air defence system before departing for the Continent in July.

On the night of 3-4 March 1945, at the eleventh hour, the Luftwaffe launched Operation Gisela, sending 140 intruders over England. They attacked fourteen bomber bases and destroyed nineteen bombers on airfields North and South of the Humber. A smaller follow-on raid was attempted on the next night, the two attacks costing the Luftwaffe around twenty aircraft. In the second raid, a Junkers Ju 88G-6 of 13/NJG 3 was shot down at 01.51 at Sutton-on-Derwent during an attack on Elvington. It was the last German aircraft to be brought down on British soil.

There is a postscript. On 10 April, 1945, a German reconnaissance aircraft of Fernaufklarungsgruppe 33 took off from Stavanger, in Norway. It made a high-level photographic run over Scapa Flow naval base, then flew south as far as the Firth of Tay before returning to its airfield. It was not intercepted.

The aircraft was an Arado 234 jet. And so, literally in the shape of things to come, the Reichsluftwaffe flew its last sortie over the North, and indeed over the British Isles.

A Broad Margin - The Battle of Britain North of Watford

Chairman:

Those privileged to live North of the Humber will rarely concede second place to the Southerners, a fact which must be evident to all of us as we sit not a five iron away from the hallowed turf of St James's Park. Every now and again, however, it takes a native of the North East to put a little perspective to Northern chauvinism.

Dr Vincent ORANGE was born at Shildon Co Durham and began his distinguished academic career as an historian at Hull University. He is Reader in the Department of History at Canterbury University, NZ and has written a number of works on RAF leaders in WWII. His books on Park and Conningham made a major contribution to the writing of RAF history and his forthcoming work on Tedder is eagerly awaited. He offers an alternative view of the air war in WWII as it affected Northern Skies.

The first part of my title A Broad Margin, is intended to remind us of Wood and Dempster's classic account of the Battle of Britain, The Narrow Margin.(1) It first appeared in 1961 and like that other thoroughbred, the Supermarine Spitfire, has since undergone significant development modification at the hands of one of its designers. Production runs have emerged from a variety of factories, but the result is still admirable. As many of you will know, the book – together with others following in its slipstream - makes a persuasive case for the belief that only a narrow margin saved Britain from defeat in 1940. Wood and Dempster's title derives from an opinion of

Winston Churchill: 'All the great struggles of history' he wrote, 'have been won by superior will-power wresting victory in the teeth of odds or upon the narrowest margins.' Neither Churchill nor Hitler lacked will-power, but I intend to show that the struggle over Britain was actually decided by decisions that reflect an absence of thoughtful planning and effective leadership in Germany.

The second part of my title, drawing attention to the lands and seas North of Watford, is of course intended to remind us of Sherlock Holmes and the strange case involving Silver Blaze, a racehorse. You will recall the following exchange between the Master and Inspector Gregory:

'Is there any point', the Inspector asked, 'to which you would wish to draw my attention?'

'To the curious incident of the dog in the night-time', replied Holmes.

'The dog did nothing in the night-time.'

'That was the curious incident.'(2)

It is an equally curious incident that there was in fact no Battle of Britain North of Watford, neither in the night-time nor in the day-time, neither in 1940 nor, more dangerously, in 1941 or 1942. There were intermittent raids in all three years, but no systematic battle. I propose to argue, from a German point of view, that a properly planned campaign, combining the striking power of escorted heavy bombers and U-boats in this region, might well have eliminated Wood and Dempster's narrow margin and given Hitler yet another victory - one that would have left his regime permanently secure from external assault.

Certainly, the geographical margin between the British Isles and the Continent is very narrow in the area from which the major attack was mounted and that fact played a significant part in the Battle's outcome in these three ways, all of which helped Hitler. Firstly, German bombers, operating from French bases, carried less fuel and more bombs to England. Secondly, their escort fighters - even though short-ranged and unwisely deprived of drop-tanks - had sufficient fuel to spend at least some time in combat with defending fighters. And thirdly, those defenders had little time either to find and engage bombers before they reached their targets or pursue them before they reached a safe distance across the Channel on the way home.

No more than 25 miles lie between Dover and Calais, but North of that strait the margin broadens rapidly. As it broadens, so the intensity of conflict declined and that, too, is a significant factor in the Battle's outcome in these three ways, none of which helped Hitler. Firstly, bombers carried more fuel and fewer bombs to England. Secondly, their escorts had insufficient fuel - being so unwisely deprived of drop-tanks - to spend any time in combat. And thirdly, defending fighters had more time either to find, engage or pursue attackers.

Between The Hook of Holland and Great Yarmouth, for example, lie 110 miles. Given exact navigation, that meant 220 miles, going and returning, over constantly alarming water under constantly threatening skies. This was in addition to the distance to be flown over land, from a German base in Holland to a target in Eastern England (assuming Great Yarmouth itself to be scarely worth bombing). German bombers of 1940, all twin-engined, had at best an economical cruising speed of 180 mph and an effective operational radius, again at best, of about 500 miles when carrying no more than 2,000 lbs of bombs - hardly a devastating load. That meant spending about 75 minutes over the North Sea, consuming nearly a quarter of the available flying time. It also meant attacking unescorted because the Luftwaffe's only effective fighter lacked the endurance necessary to accompany bombers throughout a raid inland from Great Yarmouth, let alone over regions farther North. Evasive action - either to avoid British fighters, flak at the coast or over the target or bad weather - might increase the time spent over the sea and would certainly increase fuel consumption dramatically.

From the German island of Heligoland (off the Danish coast) to Hull, the margin triples to 330 miles: 220 minutes over even more alarming water under even more threatening skies because even less fighter escort was possible. The sea passage alone took as much as two-thirds of the available flying time - and more than that in the likely event of the raid being intercepted and evasion becoming necessary. From Stavanger (near the South-west tip of Norway) to Newcastle, the margin broadens to a prohibitive 385 miles: 260 minutes over the sea, taking more than threequarters of the time available, if everything went exactly as planned. To attack Aberdeen from Stavanger was not quite impossible, but still required 205 minutes out of land sight and absorbed 62 per cent of the time available.[3]

In other words, the Luftwaffe faced insuperable problems North of Watford in 1940 and opposition that proved too strong South of that border town. Lightly loaded, medium-range, insufficiently escorted bombers were at the mercy of a carefully organised defensive system, co-ordinating the virtues of fighters, flak and barrage balloons, and provided with adequate early warning of their approach. In those circumstances, German bombers were more of a danger to their own crews than to the industrial-commercial-military strength and civilian morale of northern Britain. Nor must we forget (airmen never did) that even in daylight North Sea weather is rarely clear or calm for long. Navigational error, compounding minor damage or engine failure, would often prove as fatal as enemy attack. As for night raids, they required equipment and skills not then widely available.

In order to conquer Britain, therefore, Hitler needed to plan his attack at least as thoughtfully as Britain's defence was planned. For several years before 1940, many Britons had been anticipating an attack either direct from German bases or from any territory captured by Germans in the event of war. Given the necessary ingredients – such as clever aircraft designers, energetic manufacturers, able scientists, alert airmen, patriotic citizens and active government support – a strong defensive system was created. At the same time, those Britons who favoured the creation of a heavy bomber force capable of delivering 'a knockout blow' to Germany (if the very existence of the force did not serve as a compelling deterrent) carried on with labours that would one day fulfil their dreams.

Meanwhile, for several years before 1940, Hitler had been preparing attacks upon his neighbours, East and West. Given exactly the same ingredients – clever designers, energetic manufacturers, able scientists, alert airmen, patriotic citizens and active government support – a powerful weapon to support land armies was created. Unfortunately for Germany, those who favoured the creation of a heavy bomber force capable of delivering knockout blows either to Britain or the Soviet Union would never see their dreams fulfilled. Nor would those who believed that only a large U-boat fleet could isolate Britain and so weaken her resistance to aerial attack. These failures, together with sensible and energetic leadership on the Allied side and increasingly senseless and lethargic leadership by Hitler, determined the outcome of the war.

Luftwaffe commanders got the air force they planned, one that gave excellent service in support of land armies, but it proved incapable either of fighting a battle North of Watford or later of destroying the Soviet Union's newly emerging armament factories East of the fighting fronts. Fighter Command got its planned defensive system, equally excellent in protecting the South and East coasts of Britain. But equally incapable of operating successfully when attempting tasks for which it was neither trained nor equipped: namely, hitting the Luftwaffe so hard in the Western parts of Occupied Europe that Hitler would be obliged to withdraw air strength either from his Eastern or Mediterranean fronts.

We know now that an invasion of the British Isles was not high among Hitler's priorities in the Thirties. Recovering the Rhineland, union with Austria, dismembering Czechoslovakia, eliminating Poland and conquering France: these were his initial goals. Then would follow his ultimate goal: a joyful crusade, triumphantly fought in God's name with maximum cruelty, to sweep into oblivion a Godless, Jewish-led Bolshevik regime East of Poland. Millions of Germans, Hitler declared, so crammed together at home that they could barely exist, would expand into rich lands - some ideal for grain or cattle, others full of iron or oil - all provided with ample slave labour. These were the stuff of which Hitler's sweetest dreams were made.

It has therefore been argued that neither Britain nor her empire had anything to fear from Hitler's aggression. Germany was a land power, Britain a sea power; the elephant and the whale do not threaten each other. In any case, Hitler admired the ruthless means by which the empire had been acquired the confident rhetoric expounded to justify it and the evident determination to retain it. We 'Aryans', he mused, ought jointly to rule the world's lesser breeds. There were highly placed persons in British public life to whom Hitler's dreams also appealed or at least seemed irresistible: Chamberlain, Halifax, Lloyd George, Beaverbrook, Butler, Dunglass and scores of others who later adjusted their sentiments. The Duke and Duchess of Windsor were only too eager to move into an SS-guarded Buckingham Palace and give a royal blessing to the triumph of good sense. Had it not been for the vigorous opposition of one exceptional man - Winston Churchill - their seductive voices would, I believe, have prevailed in May or June 1940, before the Battle of Britain even began and no-one would now know of the Luftwaffe's incapacity North of Watford or the Kriegsmarine's shortage of U-boats.

Churchill's opposition to Hitler was founded in part upon his objection to brutal aggression; in part also upon his recognitions that that aggression would not end even if Hitler's armies conquered the whole of the Soviet Union and German settlers occupied every desirable acre. It is here, in my opinion, that recent revisionists are mistaken in arguing that Britain should have made peace with Hitler either before the battle or, at latest, in June 1941, after the attempt in March to protect Greece from German conquest had failed so catastrophically and before the holy crusade against the Beast in the East began. A peace was undoubtedly available that would, on paper, have guaranteed the independence of both Britain and her empire.

The alternative was alarming. Once the winter of 1940-41 was over, the Luftwaffe could be expected to return in daylight with months of good fighting weather stretching ahead, refreshed, re-equipped with improved aircraft, better organised, more experienced, more skilfully led and larger than ever. Fighter Command would be stronger too, but the narrow margin of 1940 had been achieved against a hastily improvised attack, lasting only a few weeks. A thoroughly planned attack, lasting for many weeks, might see that margin disappear. Moreover, both Dowding and Park were gone and by March 1941 there were already good grounds for fearing that their successors, Sholto Douglas and Leigh-Mallory, would handle a major battle less ably. The new commanders preferred operational flying over enemy territory to operational training over friendly territory and regarded Fighter Command as an offensive rather than defensive weapon. Many of the best pilots had been killed, wounded or captured. Others had been transferred to training duties or posted overseas. The survivors, including men rushed into the front line to meet a desperate crisis, were in need of intensive training. How do you cope with - or carry out - a surprise attack, for example; how do you regain formation after a combat?[(4)]

Before the Battle of Britain began, it had been argued, what was the point of fighting on? The entire Continent was either conquered or cowed and Britain's only potential ally of significant industrial or commercial weight, the United States, lacked both military and aviation strength at that time. Its powerful navy, based mainly in the Pacific, was more concerned about Japanese than German intentions. Wisely, therefore, the United States remained neutral.

While the night Blitz following the day battle was raging, the question bore repetition: what was the point of fighting on? Despite those commentators who so calmly pronounce it 'strategically unimportant', the Blitz was a terrible experience for Britons. On the night of 10-11 May 1941, for instance, the Luftwaffe carried out its 86th raid on London alone and by the end of that month had dropped

54,000 tons of bombs on Britain. From all causes, accidents as well as combats, it had lost no more than 600 bombers in eight months: that means two or three a day, a mere 1.5 per cent of all sorties. By the end of May, nearly 45,000 British civilians had been killed and another 50,000 seriously injured. Not until three years of war had passed did the number of British servicemen killed or injured by the Germans pass the number of civilian casualties. More than a million houses had been destroyed or damaged: that is, one out of every thirteen in Britain. All this in spite of the fact that the offensive had been neither well directed nor concentrated on vital targets: perhaps as many as threequarters of the bombs dropped had missed their designated targets altogether.(5)

Nevertheless, the bold decision to fight on in 1940 was not seriously questioned in 1941. In the short term, Britain suffered. In the long term, Hitler was overthrown and so too was a bestial regime in Tokyo. Nothing in my professional life angers me more deeply than the bleat that 'our old enemies have prospered since their defeat', overlooking the vital fact that they are now shorn of rulers who were among the most criminal ever to have infested this planet. This wonderful result was achieved in unavoidable association with an equally foul regime, but Stalin, his lackeys and the state they built are also gone. The world will face grave problems in 2095, let alone 1995, but I hope that our descendants will never be so severely tested as those most gallant men and women who directed, fought, laboured and suffered in the Allied cause during the Second World War.

This 'wonderful result', the overthrow of Hitler and his Japanese allies (not forgetting those who joined them openly or silently supported them), would have been jeopardised if a properly planned battle had been fought North of Watford in 1940; worse still, in 1941 or 1942. Three essential weapons, all available to Hitler, were not developed quickly enough in sufficient quantity. They were the U-boat, the four-engined bomber and the long-range escort fighter. Even when these gifts had been ignored, a bonus was offered: the deadly flying bomb. You may know a fine uplifting painting, perhaps Pre-Raphaelite, of a man scrabbling in a rubbish dump while behind him stands an angel offering the gift of eternal bliss, if only he will turn round and accept it. Hitler never turned round either and so failed to see the war god offering a present more certain than eternal bliss: earthly victory.

One of these divine presents was the U-boat. This weapon, as Hitler should have known, brought Germany to within a 'narrow margin' of victory during the Great War. With more boats at sea in the critical year of 1917, manufactured out of the precious steel tied up in great ships that rarely put to sea and crewed by skilled, patriotic seamen wasting away on those ships, Germany could have completed the isolation of Britain from essential imports of food and raw materials. She might also have prevented - or at least greatly delayed - transit across the Atlantic of huge numbers of American soldiers and airmen to revive flagging British and French armies. During the first half of 1917, with no more than seventy boats at sea, one in four of all British merchant ships at sea was being sunk. An average of thirteen ships was lost every day in April. 'The U-boat', wrote Winston Churchill, 'was rapidly undermining not only the life of the British islands, but the foundations of the Allies' strength; and the danger of their collapse in 1918 began to loom black and imminent.'[6] A convoy system then drastically reduced losses and although the U-boat fleet remained largely intact ('foiled rather than defeated', in the words of a British Admiral), Germany was obliged to seek an Armistice in November 1918.

Together with most other Germans, Hitler pondered deeply, though unintelligently, upon the causes of this defeat. There was no 'stab in the back', as he so vehemently asserted, by socialists, communists or Jews: the stab came in the front, from a stronger opponent who made fewer critical mistakes. When he came to power, fortunately for us, Hitler took little interest in nautical matters. He left them to Admiral Erich Raeder, a devout 'big ship' man, whose faith was not shaken either by the poor performance of the Kaiser's huge and expensive surface fleet, nor by the superb performance of his small and cheap submersible fleet, nor by any fear of what increasingly powerful aircraft might do to even the largest, most heavily armed and armoured warships.

Consequently, building ships took precedence over building submarines in the Thirties and Raeder used his authority to thwart Admiral Karl Doenitz, a Great War submariner who had a perfect understanding of the U-boat's essential role in any conflict with Britain. Hitler, Raeder and of course Hermann Goering, head of the Luftwaffe, quite failed to recognise in the U-boat a key to victory. As a valuable bonus, from Britain's viewpoint, Raeder, Doenitz and Goering quarrelled so bitterly that co-operation between U-boats and aircraft, a co-operation which would indeed have been 'a force multiplier', was never developed. A mere handful of converted airliners (four-engined Focke-Wulf Fw 200s, known as Condors) helped the boats, though never in that systematic fashion we suppose to be a Teutonic characteristic. The Condor performed amazingly well, earning its other name, 'the Scourge of the Atlantic', but it was actually a most fragile machine, a fact which wonderfully concentrated the minds of crews patrolling far from land. Any heavy landing readily broke its back and it may be that some crews were not distraught when this happened. With even fifty sturdily built, long-range aircraft, equipped with radios permitting them to direct a large pack of U-boats into the path of convoys making for British ports, Doenitz's victory would have been certain.

In fact, during the vital first year of the war, it was unusual for there to be more than eight boats at sea at any given moment. On 28 September 1939, Doenitz told Hitler: 'I am convinced that in the U-boat we have, and always have had, a weapon capable of dealing Britain a mortal blow at her most vulnerable spot.' Given 300 boats, he concluded, 'decisive success' would be achieved.(7) Even with half that number available before 1942 he would have triumphed, especially if they had been armed with reliable torpedoes that exploded when and where intended. As Harry Hinsley, Britain's official intelligence historian, wrote: 'It was only by the narrowest of margins that . . . the U-boat campaign failed to be decisive in 1941'.(8)

Winston Churchill therefore had good reason to reflect in his memoirs: 'The only thing that ever really frightened me during the war was the U-boat peril.'(9) Properly supported by Hitler, Doenitz would have turned Churchill's fear into a nightmare. As early as the night of 13-14 October 1939, for example, a single U-boat penetrated the fleet anchorage at Scapa Flow in the Orkneys – helped by an excellent set of aerial photographs supplied by the Luftwaffe – and sank the battleship Royal Oak, killing 833 officers and men. Two days later came the first aerial attack of the war upon British territory, a raid by nine twin-engined Junkers Ju 88 bombers on shipping at Rosyth in the Firth of Forth. Two cruisers were damaged and one destroyer at a cost of two bombers. The main fleet promptly withdrew to Lock Ewe, on the north-west coast of Scotland, where it would remain for the next five months, unable to help protect any target threatened from across the North Sea.(10)

What a splendid victory for one U-boat and nine unescorted

medium bombers in four days! How great would have been the victory of, say, a score of boats and fifty well-escorted heavy bombers? Imagine a campaign sustained for several weeks against the Shetlands, the Orkneys, Aberdeen and all those ports and factories lining river banks from the Tay southward to the Humber. Few U-boat captains had the exceptional skill necessary to get inside Scapa, but all were perfectly capable of keeping that great naval base and the ports farther South closed. As for bomber crews, they naturally prefer coastal targets to any other because they are easier to find and require little penetration of enemy territory.

We hope the British response to this challenge would have been effective, but it may have been as shambolic as the expedition to Norway in April 1940. In any case, it seems certain that stronger British forces - air, sea and land - would have been moved northward, leaving the vital South-East less well defended and therefore more vulnerable to German attack. Defences spread are defences weakened, as Duke William of Normandy demonstrated in 1066. The only Continental tyrant (at the time of writing) to have conquered Britain did so because the better part of the defences were exhausted in a battle North of Watford. Luckily for us, Hitler read more about American cowboys who never existed than about Medieval rulers who did. If King Harold had not been obliged to march his army from the Sussex coast to a field near York to oppose an invasion from Norway, Duke William's forces would probably have been defeated on their landing beaches – if they had attempted a landing at all.

A second present ignored by Hitler was the four-engined aircraft: both as a convoy-spotting partner for his U-boats and as a weapon capable of bombing British targets across the broad margin of the North Sea. But Hitler took as little interest in aviation matters as he did in nautical matters, leaving them to Goering, whose management proved so inept - within the Luftwaffe, the aircraft industry and in relations with other services - that I believe he was in fact a British agent! Nevertheless, the early years were promising. On Goering's recommendation, Hitler appointed a brilliant aviation organiser, Erhard Milch, as Secretary of State for Air as soon as he came to power and Milch in turn picked an outstanding army officer, Walther Wever, to be head of the Luftwaffe, once he had created it.

In 1935, Milch and Wever agreed that a heavy bomber would be needed. 'It must be able to fly right round Britain', said Milch, 'under combat conditions.'(11) By the end of 1936, two well-designed prototypes were flying, the Dornier Do 19 and the Junkers Ju 89. One or both, wrote Wood and Dempster, 'could have formed the backbone of the world's first strategic bomber fleet – and in time for the air war over Britain in 1940.'[12] Tragically for Germany, Wever was killed in a flying accident in June 1936, Milch and Goering fell out and both prototypes were cancelled by Goering.

It was a perfectly correct decision - provided Hitler never intended an attack on Britain or the Soviet Union. Big bombers were obviously more costly than medium bombers from every point of view: precious materials, skilled labour, construction time, hangar space, maintenance hours and crew size. Hardly battlefield weapons, they would be of little use in the proposed conquest of Poland, though their absence might well have embarrassed Hitler if France had not folded so rapidly. But he always had in mind an Eastern crusade and such weapons were certain to be of value in that huge territory, even if an understanding were reached with Britain.

Contrary to some claims, everything needed to build a powerful heavy bomber force was available in Germany. One sees this from the numerous projects so lightly begun and so casually continued throughout the war, few of which produced any reliable aircraft in squadron service. Add to this enormous waste the unbelievable waste of resources on rockets – whitest of the war's many white elephants, ours as well as theirs – and one must, I suggest, conclude that a thoughtful plan, vigorously implemented, would have put many strategic bombers into the air. Milch had the capacity to devise and carry through such a programme. Employed by Churchill, Roosevelt or Stalin, he would have done so, for all three proved more ruthless than Hitler when faced with servants who failed to perform; by 1941, if not before, Goering would have been out.

Systematically developed and produced in quantity, heavy bombers could have led a most destructive assault on Britain North of Watford because they would have had sufficient range to cope with that broad margin of sea which I mentioned earlier. They would also have carried enough bombs to cause severe damage to industrial and commercial targets as well as private dwellings. Machines comparable to the Avro Lancaster – that is, with an economical cruising speed of 180 mph and an effective operational radius of about 875 miles when carrying 4,000 lbs of bombs[13] – would have transformed the strategic situation. Had the Germans been able to threaten targets between Hull and Aberdeen regularly in strength from bases in

Holland, Denmark and Norway in 1940 and 1941, Fighter Command's strength could not have remained concentrated in south-eastern England. Its short-range interceptors would have performed less effectively over the broad margin and the radar chain, requiring more equipment and more operators (both in short supply at that time), and faced with much more space between them and the enemy, would have been harder pressed to give early and accurate warning.

In the middle of 1938, one year after the two heavy bombers had been scrapped, Ernst Udet decided that such a weapon was needed after all and for once he was right. Goering had put this marvellous pilot in charge of the Luftwaffe's technical development despite his technical ignorance and administrative incompetence. The new machine, a Heinkel He 177, was under construction in 1939: early enough for squadron service in 1941 if everyone concerned had acted sensibly and urgently. Sadly, an excellent design was ruined by two of Udet's most stupid decisions: its four engines were coupled in two nacelles and its airframe was sufficiently strengthened, in theory, to permit diving attacks by an aircraft weighing at least thirty tons. As a result, when the engines didn't catch fire, the wings came off. Or vice versa. Sometimes only the tail assembly disintegrated.

'How is such an engine to be serviced on the airfields?' Goering asked in May 1942. 'I believe I am right in saying you cannot even take out all the sparking plugs without pulling the whole engine apart!' A version with its four engines mounted separately was planned in 1940, but not flown until late in 1943. As for the diving capacity, 'It is straightforward idiocy', Goering said, 'to ask of a four-engined bomber that it should dive.' Only too true, but his objection should have been voiced some three years earlier, while the machine was being built. No other air commander, ancient or modern, can have been quite so slack when it came to acquiring facts about his inventory as opposed to making extravagant claims for its quality and quantity to Hitler and the trusting German public. Milch told Goering in October 1942 that the coming year would see a crushing Anglo-American bomber offensive by night and day, but Goering disagreed. There was 'no cause for anxiety', he replied: 'we can contemplate the future with equanimity.'[(14)]

In order to protect their strategic bombers, the Germans would have needed a long-range, single-engined fighter and it too – third of the presents spurned by Hitler – was available long before the war. The Heinkel He 112 was one of four contenders at a competition held in October 1935. It and the Messerschmitt Bf 109 outclassed the other two. Both machines flew with the same British engine - a Rolls-Royce Kestrel V – which greatly assisted fair comparison. In level flight the Messerschmitt proved slightly faster, but the Heinkel had a better rate of climb, a smaller turning circle and was nearly as agile. Its large, deep cockpit was more comfortable and gave the pilot a better view; a wide-track undercarriage made ground handling safer; it was larger and more strongly built (permitting easier installation of heavy armament) and – not least – it had a much longer range. Although test pilots preferred the Heinkel, the Messerschmitt was cheaper and easier to mass produce and got the nod.

After the rejection of his fighter, Heinkel undertook a complete structural overhaul, producing in the 112B a virtually new aircraft. The fuselage had a better aerodynamic shape and was much lighter. The production prototype first flew in July 1937 and was 25 mph faster than the Bf 109B-1, equipped with a similar engine. Even so, the Luftwaffe received excellent service from the Messerschmitt in all its models throughout the war and I do not suggest that it should have been dropped. The Luftwaffe, in my opinion, needed both machines. Their qualities, like those of the British Hurricane and Spitfire, were complementary. In range, robust construction, weight of armament and ability to carry drop-tanks, the Heinkel had a distinct advantage; in agility and high altitude performance, the Messerschmitt was superior.

The German mistake was to prefer the twin-engined Messerschmitt Bf 110 to the Heinkel. Optimistically designated 'the Destroyer' by Goering, it served indifferently as a fighter, bomber escort and ground attacker. Only in a role for which it had not been intended - that of night-fighter - did it achieve success. The Heinkel would have proved a much better partner for the 109 than the heavy, clumsy machine actually employed in that role with disastrous consequences during the Battle of Britain. So far from partnering the 109 against Hurricanes and Spitfires, the destroyer needed an escort itself.

Although the He 112 would have served admirably as a frontline fighter, its successor - the He 100 - would have performed better still. Drawings were complete by the end of May 1937 for an aircraft originally designated 113. Fifteen examples of the D version were built between March and September 1939. Despite out-performing its Messerschmitt equivalent, it was not taken into Luftwaffe service. Its airframe was closely tailored to the Daimler-Benz 601 engine, but production of that engine was almost totally absorbed by the 109 and the Destroyer. The Air Ministry, at that time happy with Messerschmitt's duo, instructed Heinkel to concentrate on his twin-engined bomber, then in mass production.

Russian and Japanese delegations visited Heinkel in October 1939 to examine the 100D. The Russian delegation included Alexander Yakovlev, designer of the Yak-1, which had appeared earlier that year, and purchased six examples of Heinkel's fighter. Yakovlev made good use of them in producing improved versions of his own basic design, particularly the Yak-9 (in large-scale production by August 1942) and the Yak-3 (which appeared a year later). As for the Japanese, they bought three 100Ds and a DB 601 engine. With these to inspire them, they produced the Kawasaki 'Hien' (Swallow), named 'Tony' by the Americans. Early in 1942, the Swallow was tested against a captured Curtiss P-40E and an imported Bf 109E. It proved markedly superior to both and would serve with distinction for two years as the standard Japanese Army Air Force Fighter.

Meanwhile, a few 100Ds were used by the Germans for propaganda photographs in a variety of markings to give the impression that they were in large-scale production. Described as 'Heinkel 113s', they deceived Allied Intelligence for a long time. The He 113 was frequently reported in action during the Battle of Britain when in fact it took no part at all. The laugh, however, was really on the Germans because this formidable machine, serving instead of the so-called Destroyer, might well have converted the narrow margin by which the Luftwaffe was defeated into a victory with incalculable consequences.(15)

As you know, the gods are tolerant of human kind (they need to be) and grant us a bonus gift, no matter how unwisely we use the statutory three. On their behalf, therefore, the war god offered Hitler a last chance, the flying bomb. Like the U-boat, the four-engined bomber and the long-range fighter, the V-1 (as it came to be known) was another key to victory which Hitler failed to grasp. It was small, fast, cheap, unmanned and difficult to intercept even by the best pilots in Fighter Command, mounted on the fastest, most heavily armed machines. Once launched, as Jozef Garlinski wrote, it 'can no longer be steered; it is kept on its course by an automatic pilot and moved forward by its own impulsion. It is in reality a miniature submarine without a crew.'(16) Although it could not take evasive action; it never flinched when attacked nor did it worry about the journey home across even the broadest margin of sea.

Around 1935, the Argus aero-engine firm invented a pulse-jet, but nothing whatever was done to exploit it until as late as April 1942, when Hitler ordered 'terror attacks' on British cities in reprisal for the destruction of Lubeck. Argus was ordered to develop the jet; Fieseler to design and produce an airframe; Askania to make a control mechanism and Walter a launching ramp. Erhard Milch gave the work a high priority in June, but no-one ensured that these companies actually co-operated with maximum enthusiasm, pooling all their skills. Nevertheless, the first flight took place on Christmas Eve and this dangerous weapon ought to have been readily available in ample numbers a year later, by the end of 1943.

As ever, fortunately, Hitler failed to snatch a truly war-winning weapon from the war god's hand and then insist upon urgent, systematic development and production. Year after year, he tolerated - in this and other matters - poor co-operation between armament firms, bitter inter-service rivalry and political interference to a degree unmatched in the states ruled by Churchill, Roosevelt and Stalin. Better still, from our point of view, he permitted enormous resources in scarce material and highly skilled manpower to be expended on an Army project, a supersonic rocket, the V-2: a vastly more expensive and technically difficult weapon. If it worked properly, which sometimes happened, it delivered a one-ton explosion: no greater than that delivered by the Luftwaffe's project, the flying bomb, at a fraction of the cost. About 30,000 bombs were produced, of which 3,500 eluded Britain's defences. We may well wonder what Hitler might have achieved with double that number on hand even a few weeks before they actually began to hit England on 13 June 1944, one week after D-Day.

As you also know, the gods' gifts contain a fatal fish-hook, activated if they are improperly used. In Hitler's case, the fish-hook was time. War has always been the most unpredictable as well as the most dangerous and expensive option that any state can choose. Having himself endured four years of the bloodiest war in European history, Hitler had compelling reasons to consider his objectives carefully. To overcome his immediate neighbours required a large, well-equipped army, closely supported by fighters and bombers, none of which needed a long range. But to overcome huge empires, one centred on London, the other on Moscow, required additional weapons and plenty of them. He failed to decide which were essential and then ensure that these and no others were urgently developed and produced. He was not pressed for time. No state in the world threatened him. On the contrary, all were concerned to appease him, especially those which ultimately destroyed him. He had no need to begin a war until he was ready. Ready not merely for a short war, but for a long one. As far back as the human record goes, it has never been wise to assume that one's enemies will crumple as quickly as one hopes. Much better to assume that they are strong and so act that one destroys them utterly or enslaves them permanently. Hitler had at his disposal everything necessary to do this, except patience, judgement and leadership: that capacity which Churchill, Roosevelt and Stalin had to ensure that their subordinates, in and out of uniform, co-operated with each other most of the time and gave most of their attention to winning the war.

It is easy now to see that Hitler lost a war he could have won before the Allies summoned up the strength and determination to win it. Time was slipping from his side, but did not quite abandon him until the end of 1941. By then, he had failed to topple the Soviet regime, thanks to the strategy he imposed upon his Generals and the cruelty he demanded of his soldiers. By then also, he had gratuitously added the United States to his list of enemies. Time that could have been spent producing U-boats, heavy bombers, long-range fighters and flying bombs: weapons with which to stave off the conquest of Germany even if her conquests were gradually lost.

Time to increase the bomb's range (initially, a mere 160 miles) in order to threaten Britain North of Watford. Time to develop further the highly promising tactic of launching it from conventional aircraft and so threatening ports, factories, harbours and airfields in every corner of Britain. Time, above all, to hammer Britain before D-Day, when it was said that the island was so full of tanks, trucks, aircraft, soldiers and airmen that only the barrage balloons prevented it from sinking beneath the waves. In the face of such an attack, these forces must have been dispersed and the landings in Normandy made even more difficult to establish ashore. And finally time after D-Day, to saturate the small Normandy bridgehead and the supply lines running to it. From late in 1943, British and American bombers heavily attacked such launching sites as were discovered in Occupied Europe, but nothing they did could have prevented a devastating bombardment of Britain if in 1942 Hitler had insisted upon urgent development and production of flying bombs. As it was, a great many first-class British fighters, that could have made life easier and safer for the Allied soldiers ashore, were employed solely against missiles, just as a great weight of Allied bombs, that could have made life even harder and less safe for Germans in their homeland, were dropped instead on launching sites, actual and suspected, in Occupied Europe.[17]

The 'Broad Margin' of my title, then, is not the water separating Hitler from the British Isles, but the time which he had to cross that water and so fecklessly wasted.

1. Derek Wood with Derek Dempster, *The Narrow Margin: The Battle of Britain and the Rise of Air Power, 1930-1940* (Hutchinson, London, 1961; latest ed., Tri-Service Press, London, 1990).
2. Arthur Conan Doyle, *Silver Blaze* in *The Penguin Complete Sherlock Holmes* (Penguin, London, 1981) p. 347. The story appears in numerous other editions.
3. US Defense Mapping Agency, *Digital Chart of the World:* distance information provided by Janet Bray, Geography Department, University of Canterbury. On aircraft performance see Alfred Price, *The Bomber in World War II* (Macdonald and Jane's, London) and the appendices in Wood and Dempster.
4. Vincent Orange, 'After the Battle of Britain: Fighter Command, September 1940 to December 1941' (unpublished paper).
5. Winston G. Ramsey (ed.), *The Blitz Then and Now* (Battle of Britain Prints International, London, 1988) vol. 2, p. 627.
6. John Terraine, *Business in Great Waters: The U-Boat Wars, 1916-1945* (Leo Cooper, London, 1989) pp. 46-7.
7. Terraine, *Business*, pp. 218-219.
8. F. H. Hinsley (and others), *British Intelligence in the Second World War: Its Influence on Strategy and Operations* (HMSO, London, 1981) vol. 2, p. 169.
9. Winston Churchill, *The Second World War, Volume Two: Their Finest Hour* (Cassell, London, 1949) p. 472.
10. Ramsey, *Blitz,* vol. 1, pp. 37-39; Terraine, *Business*, pp. 222-223 (where 309 men lost is a mistake for 809); Richard Hough and Denis Richards, *The Battle of Britain* (Coronet Books, London, 1989) pp. 68-69.
11. David Irving, *The Rise and Fall of the Luftwaffe: The Life of Luftwaffe Marshal Erhard Milch* (Futura Publications, London, 1976) p. 35.
12. Wood and Dempster, *Narrow Margin*, p. 21.
13. Price, *Bomber*, p. 98.
14. Irving, *Rise and Fall,* pp. 169-173.
15. Vincent Orange, 'Fortunate Fascist Failures: The Case of the Heinkel Fighters' in *Historical News* (University of Canterbury, 1983) pp. 7-13.
16. Jozef Garlinski, *Hitler's Last Weapons: The Underground War against the V-1 and V-2* (Magnum Books, London, 1979) p.8.
17. Basil Collier, *The Defence of the United Kingdom* (HMSO, London, 1957) pp. 338-340, 353-397; Alfred Price, 'V-Weapons' in I. C .B. Dear and M. R. D. Foot (eds.), *The Oxford Companion to the Second World War* (Oxford University Press, 1995) pp. 1249-1253.

From Spitfire & Mosquito to Hunter & Javelin

Chairman:

The committee of the Society has made a top priority for its future programmes the move into the period following WWII, about which very little has been said or written. A very strong team has come together for this seminar, to address the post war period when, for the second time in less than 30 years, a massive dismantling of forces was begun. This was only to be reversed in the face of a flexing of communist muscles in places as far apart as Berlin and Korea. Part of the reversal demanded the tackling of a substantial technological deficit, in order to take the RAF properly into the jet age.

AM Sir Peter BAIRSTO had a distinguished career in the Royal Air Force, culminating in his appointment as an unforgettable Chief of Staff at Strike Command in the mid 1980s. His credentials for addressing the immediate past are impeccable for he served as a flight commander on No. 43 Sqn. at Leuchars in the 50s and, later, commanded No. 66 Sqn. at Acklington. He has experience of air defence at all levels and was intimately involved in Fighter Command in the early days of the jet age.

My subject is the air defence of the UK North of the Humber, in the period from the end of World War II to 1960. In part of that period I was flying the Meteor, F86 (Sabre) and Hunter Mk 1-9 day fighters, and was a Flight and Squadron Commander in 13 Group. I also flew the Vampire, Meteor NF11 and 14 and Javelin elsewhere.

I begin with the evolution of the air defence fighter force in the UK from the end of World War II until it reached its peak around 1957. I shall deal with the period in 4 phases:

First, the end of World War II to 1946. The post war contraction of Fighter Command really began before the end of the war, as the fighting in North West Europe moved steadily eastwards. By the end of hostilities in Europe in May 1945, of the 8 Groups in the Command which had covered the whole of the UK, only two, 11 and 12 Groups, were on full status, defending the country East and South of a line joining Cape Wrath, Banbury and St. Davids, the remainder of the UK and Northern Ireland being a Shadow Area. By December 1946, the Command's front line strength was 192 aircraft in 18 day fighter squadrons equipped at 8 AE with a mixed bag of Vampire, Meteor and Hornet day fighters, and 6 night fighter squadrons equipped to the same cadre level with the Mosquito. None of these squadrons was based North of Linton-on-Ouse.

Now, 1946 to 1948. A Directive to the AOC-in-C Fighter Command in December 1946 said that for the next two years the Command should concentrate on research and experiment in air defence as first priority, and providing air defence for the maximum areas which could be manned effectively. Stress was laid on attaining the highest possible interception rate by day and night irrespective of weather; on raid reporting and fighter control organisation, and on standardisation of operational and training techniques to permit rapid reinforcement of the Command in an emergency by fighter squadrons from Germany. This Directive was based on a Defence Planning Assumption that there would be no further conflict for at least 10 years. This assumption had the economic advantage of a slower rate of expenditure and making maximum use of existing aircraft, equipment and weapons. It also meant that the mixed bag of aircraft which appeared during the latter stages of the war, to which I have already referred, would not be replaced until about 1957. Much of what was going on in this period was overshadowed by manpower contraction, as an airforce over a million strong was being demobilised to something like 300,000 all ranks, with extensive demands for our aircraft and manpower in Germany, the Mediterranean, the Middle East, India and the Far East, and with preoccupations with colonial problems like that in Palestine. The only significant improvement in operational capability in this period, in terms of aircraft numbers, was the reformation from June 1946 onwards of 20 Auxiliary squadrons, equipped with piston aircraft under Fighter Command Operational Control, but in Home Command. Some of these part time squadrons did have the great advantage of being based North of the Humber at such places as Thornaby, Aldergrove, Ouston, Abbotsinch, Turnhouse and Dyce.

Thirdly, 1948 to 1956. I come now to probably the most significant period in the history of the defence of the North of the UK, 1948 to 1956. It was in 1948 that the realities of burgeoning East-West tension dawned on the Government, due to the sudden Russian blockade of Berlin, and the invasion of South Korea by Chinese backed Communists in the North. As a consequence, Parliament was told that production of the latest types of jet interceptor was to be doubled and reconditioning of older types of fighter accelerated. Air defences were to be improved with new equipment, whilst the overhaul of stocks of wartime material still of use with later types of aircraft was authorised. The key position of fighter squadrons in the defence of Britain made it also important to bring the Auxiliary squadrons up to strength; re-equipment of its squadrons with jet aircraft was to be completed as soon as possible. With the Meteor and Vampire already in service, the day fighter force was comparatively well placed for expansion, but prospects for modernising the night fighter force were less promising. Wartime experience showed that two-seater night fighters were essential and a specification had been issued early in 1948 for an all weather jet aircraft to be in service as soon as possible, later to be incarnated as the Javelin. If the night fighter force were to remain effective until such a type came into service, a stop-gap would have to be introduced and it was thus decided to proceed with a night fighter version of the Meteor. With the tempo of events beginning to quicken, a new Directive to the AOC-in-C Fighter Command in August 1949 reflected the urgency of the situation. In contrast to the previous one, which was concerned with research and experiment in air defence and the defence of the maximum area of the United Kingdom which could be manned effectively, the new Directive stated unequivocally that the Command's operational commitment was the defence of the United Kingdom against air attack. One of a series of moves to strengthen the Command, and bring all components of the active air defence in the United Kingdom under operational control of Fighter Command by early 1956, saw the Auxiliary squadrons, all of which were now considered to have reached a sufficient standard of operational training to take their place in front line units, transferred to Fighter Command. In July 1950 the readiness state of the Command was brought to a higher pitch when a number of aircraft were put on armed alert to intercept unidentified aircraft approaching British air space. The timing of this action was significant, coming as it did when international tension was rising after the invasion of South Korea in June 1950. Also in July 1950 the Ministry of Defence revealed alarming figures on the estimated strength of the Soviet Armed Forces, whose airpower was calculated at 19,000 aircraft, including jet fighters and long range bombers, leading in August 1950 to a new three year defence plan which, at £4.7 billion was the largest peacetime defence expenditure ever authorised. There was little that could be done about strengthening the front line until production of aircraft built up, but by early 1951 Fighter Command's regular day fighter strength had been doubled and all squadrons had been equipped with jets. In November 1951, fighter strength in the UK was further increased with the arrival of an RCAF Sabre Wing at North Luffenham. Vampires were phased out of service in the United Kingdom, being completely replaced in the regular front line by Meteor 8s. This new mark fitted with an ejector seat had better range and performance than its predecessors, but the RAF still awaited a swept wing fighter – at that time only available from the United States. By December 1951 Fighter Command had reached a regular strength of 20 Meteor Mk 8 and 3 Vampire Mk 5 day fighter squadrons, and 6 night all-weather squadrons equipped variously with Meteor NF11s, Vampire NF10s and Venom NF3s, all these squadrons were at 16 or 22 AE. The 20 Auxiliary squadrons were all still at 8 AE, and equipped with a mixed bag of Vampire 3 and 5, and Meteor 4 and 8. These squadrons were located on 26 airfields, albeit only 14 were regular stations. Significantly, the only regular squadrons North of Linton-on-Ouse at this time were three which had been moved from the South to Leuchars. Meanwhile, the introduction of increasing numbers of the MIG 15 was viewed with mounting concern, particularly as the performance of the types in service with Western European airforces was inferior to that of the MIG 15. In 1950 it was thought that in about three years suitable fighters would have been developed in Europe and be in production, but the immediate problem was to meet the situation which would arise in the event of war within that period. It was appreciated that if hostilities occurred during the 1953-56 period the Russian medium bomber force – probably jet-equipped from about 1954 – would be largely engaged in attacking the United Kingdom, but tactical bombers would not be available to attack targets in Britain until after a stalemate was reached in the land campaign, probably on the Rhine. Whether the Russians reached the Channel coast or were held on the Rhine, it was assumed that UK based defences would have to meet Russian short range fighters. Hence, in late 1952 the RAF began to take on board the United States F86 Sabre (built in our case in Canada). These aircraft were located mainly in Germany, but the Linton-on-Ouse wing was re-equipped with them in December 1953. Despite some criticism at the time, it was a wise decision to introduce the Sabre as a stop gap pending the introduction of British swept-wing fighters. It gave the RAF an aircraft in the transonic class at a critical period when East-West relations were tense, since the Hunter – the first successful British swept-wing fighter, given the failure of the Swift as an air defence fighter – did not arrive in Fighter Command until the spring of 1954. So far as organisation of the Command was concerned, 81 Fighter Group was re-formed in January 1952 to control OTU and other training facilities. In April 1955, 13 Group was re-established to control the Northern and Caledonian fighter sectors.

Throughout this period a works programme was in progress developing airfields to meet the expanding fighter force requirements. To improve reaction time, operational readiness platforms (ORPs) were built at the end of main runways, enabling aircraft to be positioned for immediate take-off. These aircraft were linked by telephone or "telescramble" to their controlling authority, thus enabling the pilots at cockpit readiness to get their take-off orders direct from the controllers, and hence improving reaction time.

Finally, the remainder of the decade 1956-1960. The remainder of the decade up to 1960 saw the Hunter as Fighter Command's standard single seat day fighter; in the second half of the 1950s we progressed through the Avon powered MkI and Sapphire powered MkII, which more or less entered service together at Leuchars and Wattisham in 1955. (This was the first widely used RAF day fighter to be equipped with powered controls and its single point pressure refuelling system and detachable Aden gun pack reduced turn-round time to as little as seven minutes. The fire power conferred by the four 30mm Aden cannon – which delivered ten times as much high explosive per second as the cannon of the MiG – marked one of the major advances in the fighters' basic weapon since the 20mm Hispano came into general use in 1941.) The progression continued with the introduction by 1956 of the replacement Hunter Mk4, which had additional fuel capacity in the wings, and provision for external fuel tanks and weapons below them. Within two years the force was re-equipped with the Mk6 which had an up-rated Avon engine, giving the Hunter a much improved performance, and after another year or so some squadrons had the Mk9 with a long range ferry capability and ground attack weapons. The Meteor NF11 and later the NF14, and Venom NF2, were the mainstay of the night fighter force until the Javelin, the first delta wing fighter in the world, entered service in 11 Group, and progressively in the other Groups. The heat seeking Firestreak air-to-air guided missile was standard on the Javelin Mk7 from 1958. In January 1957 the fighter force in the UK reached its peak, with 448 day fighters in 18 Regular and 20 Auxiliary squadrons and 272 Night/All Weather fighters in 17 squadrons, with a fair number of those aircraft, and relevant exercises, focused on northern skies.

But that Spring there came a bombshell in our midst, and not from Russians coming through the Skagerrak with snow on their wings – it was what became known as the notorious Duncan Sandys Axe, which brought about a massive reduction in the UK fighter force between 1957 and 1960.

And so we come to air defence in the nuclear deterrent age. To understand why Sandys' axe fell upon the RAF in 1957, it is essential to take account of the appreciation made of the threat to the UK, and consequent equipment plans. As I explained earlier, requirements for new aircraft and equipment to come into service in the early and middle 1950s, had been drawn up shortly after the war. But by 1950 the defence situation had changed so drastically that new plans had to be made to meet a threat to the United Kingdom in the 1960-70 period. In broad terms it was appreciated that from about 1960, Russia could threaten Britain with medium range ballistic missiles (1,500 miles range) or by attacks at medium and high altitude by aircraft carrying free fall and stand-off nuclear weapons and flying at increasingly faster speeds and greater height – possibly Mach 2.5 at 70,000 ft. by 1970. Sophisticated forms of electronic countermeasures (ECM) might be used to support them. Low altitude subsonic attacks could also be expected. The defensive system to counter these threats would have to be proof against saturation by large numbers of aircraft, and the warning time had to be long enough to ensure interception at least 20 miles from the coast. Britain's geographical position behind the NATO radars gave improved warning of attack, but an adequate national early warning system was still necessary. The reporting radars in use were vulnerable to electronic countermeasures and the system was limited in the number of attack and defending aircraft it could handle. Manned fighters in the large numbers required to meet mass raids presented us with many problems of readiness, take off and recovery which tended to degrade the effectiveness of the force as a whole. The first generation SAM, due to come into service towards the end of the decade were comparatively short range, vulnerable to ECM and could only provide a limited improvement in defence if costs were to be kept within reasonable bounds. Even developed versions would not provide a complete defence. Thus, although fighter costs were markedly greater than those of SAM for a given level of defence effectiveness, the aircraft with its ability to discriminate, intercept, identify targets and report, something the SAM could not do – would still be an essential element in the defensive posture of the 1960s. Retention of the fighter also provided a safeguard against delay or cancellation in the SAM programme.

The policy was to use both aircraft and SAM in the air defence of the United Kingdom and link the C&R system to Continental radars. The Government's policy stressed that counter offensive strength was the most effective defence against aggression, which was to say that "Deterrence" was to form the basis of future British defence policy. Thus, in April 1957 the Government dramatically announced considerable cuts in the number of fighter aircraft in Britain. The V bomber and Thor missile deterrent force had, of course, been building up apace over the later 1950s, as had the Bloodhound SAM system, and it was considered essential that a would-be aggressor should not be allowed to knock-out the V Force bases before the aircraft could take off. Hence, a manned fighter force, smaller than that established in 1956, but adequate for this limited purpose in conjunction with Bloodhound – and progressively equipped with air-to-air missiles – was to be maintained until replaced by a more advanced SAM system than Bloodhound. In these circumstances it was considered unlikely the RAF would need a fighter aircraft more advanced than the Lightning, which was then within 2 or 3 years of front line service.

Once the decision was announced to recast the air defences to concentrate on bomber airfield defence, the reduction of the fighter force was rapid. In March 1957 the 20 Auxiliary squadrons were disbanded, and in December that year, two Hunter and three Venom NF squadrons had also been disbanded.

A further ten squadrons were withdrawn from the Command in the next two years, reducing established front line strength by December 1959 to 124 aircraft in ten short range day Hunter squadrons and 160 aircraft in ten night/all weather Javelin squadrons. 13 Group soon disappeared, as did 81 Operational Training Group. Most importantly, of course, by the early 1960s the air defence focus swung away from northern skies, towards central England and East Anglia where the V Force, most of the Thor force and USAF Strategic forces were based, and it was not until later in that decade that the focus again turned towards the North when it became obvious that the inbound Russian route was likely to be via the north of Norway rather than the Skagerrak.

That brings me to the end of the history lesson which I felt was important to an understanding of the extraordinary happenings in air defence in the 15 years after World War II. I have not mentioned the vital air defence ground environment, which will shortly be picked up by Alec Morris.

I turn now to some recollections of my days in 13 Group. In this context, I think it important for you to appreciate that this speaker was a Flight and Squadron commander, at Flight Lieutenant and Squadron Leader level, age group 26 to 32 years at the time, and not – as my reading of the papers of this Society's proceedings hitherto suggest to me – one of those who usually address these fora, such as the Commanders of the time, with all of the facts before them. I speak then from the worm's eye view, and apologise if, in the innocence of those days, I ruffle any feathers. I have been asked to cover a number of topics, and I do so briefly, if only to provoke discussion later.

Let me look first at the quality of leadership and training. In the early part of the expansion period I have been talking about, I was a flying instructor on Meteor Mk7s and 8s at an Advanced Flying School – believe it or not there were 10 of these Meteor and Vampire Units in the early 1950s, converting piston trained or re-tread pilots to jets. I well remember the very mixed bag of people who were in the training machine in those days: heavily be-medalled types, some coming back after 4 or 5 years in civvy street, trying to come to terms with jets after years on pistons. Many made it, of course, but others barely did so for their reactions could not be brought fully up to speed, and eventually found themselves in difficulties in the front line. Places like Driffield were a Meteor bloodbath – at Worksop, where I instructed, and was station flight safety officer, we counted upon one fatality a month. When 43 Squadron converted to the first Hunters, we had 6 serious crashes, including fatalities, in the first 6 months of the aircraft; it was said (and certainly they figured prominently in the Command Flight Safety Magazine) the first Sabre squadron at Linton-on-Ouse wrote-off 22 AE aircraft in the first 22 months. There was too much expansion and re-equipment going on at the same time, not just in Fighter Command, but also in the other 7 UK Commands and the three Commands overseas; furthermore, there were colonial wars to be dealt with, like Palestine, Kuwait, Suez and Kenya. Many of our senior people, brought up to long periods of operations with piston aircraft seemed to find it difficult to comprehend the scope and horizons of jet fighters; supervision was often not what it should have been because of inability to assimilate the essentials of the jet fighter. Cases of squadron commanders who led their chaps en route from the back of a Hastings, or could only hit the flag by flying into it, or of flight commanders who could not lead in bad weather, were common talk in crew rooms. There was, of course, an obverse to this: our flight, squadron and station commanders had been to war, had stared the enemy in the face, had kills on their belts, and scars. They gave us a strong sense of what we were about – to fight our machines, kill the enemy. Not for them expressions of fear of, or sympathy for, the enemy, which so shocked me when latterly I was at Strike Command during the Falklands War; unfortunately, some of those World War II operators did not combine the vital qualities of aggression with the ability to operate a jet aircraft to its optimum capability, and this plainly had an adverse effect at times in 13 Group.

Looking at aircraft systems and performance, I have to say the F86 Sabre was the finest aircraft I ever flew. Everything worked on it, and kept working; it had a tiny gun, but a good aiming system and magnificent manoeuvrability, particularly in the rolling plane. The Meteor had a good record at the end of World War II and in Korea; it was blessed with enough poke and weapons to do the job as a bomber destroyer in its day, but once the Canberra came along it was struggling to catch up. Like so many British aircraft, even in recent years, the Hunter was a delightful flying machine, but it was not designed around a weapons system – the latter was just stuffed in anywhere. The four Aden guns blasted hell out of the airframe, and I landed twice in succession during gunfiring trials with the nose wheel stuck up. The radar ranging device hardly ever lasted more than one sortie, even with the Command's best PAIs and Technicians looking after it; our firing results on the flag, because of endless fiddling with the radar and zeroing were not ones to shout about.

During my time in the Command, tactics were bedevilled by a number of factors. We were supposed to be devoting much of our time to bomber destroying out over the North Sea, and our Exercises were so designed, but we also had an overseas reinforcement role, where we were to be employed either in Air Defence or Close Support of Ground Troops. With our limited capability against high flying fast targets, the former occupation was seen by many as boring and repetitive, whereas ground attack was exciting and you could get good results with the Aden guns and even three inch rocket. Dog fighting, tail chasing, ground attack opportunities, and any excuse to go looking for trade (bouncing one of the other Wings out of the blue) were seized upon with alacrity, rather than performing four ninety degree interceptions, or two very doubtful off-set one eighty's for some long suffering GCI Station. The Hunter began life without enough fuel, and when it had enough this was in outboard fuel tanks which curtailed manoeuvrability. Navigation, when not within sight of ground radar, was by the seat of the pants, or by dint of rudimentary distance measuring equipment, combined later with a very dubious radio compass. This was bad enough getting around the UK, but on our overseas trips around the Mediterranean, it was often hilarious.

Life on a Hunter squadron in those days was still influenced by the combat fighter pilot "ethos" of World War II, and this tended to militate against a full blooded application to our primary role as interceptors of bombers. CFE was still studying, and in that magnificent Day Fighter Leader's School practising, the concepts of dogfighting and "many-fighters-versus-many-fighters". Of course, there was a case for dog-fighting, but from the outside looking in, I felt the night-all-weather Javelin squadrons were far more professional about the science of interception than we were. Of course, they did not have the other distractions that we had: providing the RAF aerobatic team took up a lot of time on one squadron I was in – indeed, it was made quite clear to me on more than one occasion that our performance all over Europe in this respect, was far more important than serviceable weapons systems. Six of the day fighter squadrons, including my own, also had an overseas reinforcement role and roulement commitment, and we were never so happy as when the wheels were in the well and we were on our way to some exotic Mediterranean location where, although we would have an interception role as well as a close support role, the presence of the Army and ground attack ranges soon had us doing what we enjoyed most. I am confident that we gave a very good account of ourselves at the ground attack role, but because of the limitations and, in some cases, unreliability of our systems including the GCI radars, I am not altogether sure the Russians needed to tremble about attacking the UK in the '50s. The unreliability of our systems was not always the fault of design: our hard worked engineering supervisors had a lot of National Service Airmen to cope with, hence the depth of engineering experience was not what it was when I later commanded a Wing overseas and a Station at home in an all-regular Air Force. We had some National Service pilots about, but these were mostly of a good standard despite their short stay.

When we got down to exercising in the Air Defence role, one of the things that struck me later when I moved on to encompass other roles and theatres, was the almost complete lack of Intelligence at that time, both in terms of a general understanding of the threat and also anything significantly synthetic relating to the Exercise we were about to undertake. Hence, we went into one of these exercises with nothing more than the notion that Bomber Command was going to come storming in over the North Sea at 35-40,000 feet, at some time; I do not recall that we had an adequate understanding of their likely tactics or targets. Although in the Meteor era, interceptions had been effectively carried out with close GCI control, the way the Hunters went about intercepting raiders was based on the assumption that jamming would prevent any radar controlled interceptions, so the "Loiter technique" was adopted. This involved scrambling the whole fighter force to take up and hold position about 80 miles off the coast at the start of a matrix of "loiter lanes". These lanes were about 15 miles wide, radiating in an easterly direction, and each pilot would be allocated to a particular lane. the problem was that without radar control, we had to fall back on our Distance Measuring Equipment which, theoretically allowed you to dial a station and its distance from you would show on the instrument. By dialling into two or more stations alternately you could fix your position by crude triangulation.

The problem was that each station could handle about 70 signals at a time, and since the whole of Fighter Command was trying to log in, no one could get a reading. The net result was that one was not always near the position one hoped to be at. When ground control thought the "enemy" were approaching, they would signal to the fighters to proceed down their loiter lanes (using a channel switching technique to avoid the Jamming) and we would make visual interceptions. We had successes at 35-45,000 feet, but often we turned-on too late, resulting in a stern chase which did not effect a kill until the bomber had achieved its stand-off weapon release. Early Radar Warning was, of course, of the essence in getting us to our loiter positions and off down our lanes at the right moment, and to this end our controlling Sectors depended upon links to continental radars – I do not think this was always effective. I am told that in the mid-50s four Neptune Maritime aircraft were adapted for AEW duties at Topcliffe, but they never did anything for the Northern Skies as far as I was aware. Mixed Hunter and Javelin tactics at night were trialled by one of the Hunter squadrons at Middleton St. George. I am told that with the Javelin and Hunter taking off together and the former leading the latter into the targets, this technique could be quite effective.

So, there we must leave it. The Spitfire and Mosquito to Hunter and Javelin era from World War II to 1960 was one of very rapid change, rundown after the War, expansion and contraction, overshadowed to some extent by operational concepts and leadership that were slow to catch up with the pace of aircraft performance, bedevilled by weapons systems that did not keep pace with improving aircraft performance, and with numerous inexperienced National Servicemen in our midst. That we coped, and made a contribution to our eventual victory in the Cold War, is a tribute to the flexibility that has always been a key characteristic of our service, and to our leadership, at all levels.

Type 80 Radar of the ROTOR Age

Hunter F6s of No. 92 Sqn over Cyprus, 1961

(©Crown Copyright)

Javelin FAW9s of No. 33 Sqn

Bloodhound Mk I Surface to Air Missile

Thor Intermediate Range Ballistic Missile

Lightning F1s of No. 74 Sqn

Lighting F3 of No. 29 Sqn refuelling from Victor Mk 1

Shackleton AEW2 of No. 8 Sqn RAF Lossiemouth

Phantom!

Type 91 radar of UKADGE (foreground) with (left) Type 85 and (right) HF 200 of earlier period

Tornado F3 of 111 Sqn, RAF Leuchars, 1995

UK Control & Reporting System from the End of WWII to ROTOR and Beyond

Chairman:

The need for a competent system for detection and control of air defences was well recognised from the days of Ashmore. The development of the first radars, just in time for WWII, put a massive missing piece into the jigsaw. The early post war years saw retrenchment and a withering of the defensive chain but the dawning of the Cold War soon changed that.

AM Sir Alec MORRIS joined the RAF at the end of WWII and was immediately involved in the run down of the wartime C&R system. He was involved throughout his career in AD matters and has an unrivalled knowledge of developments in the period of the ROTOR system and, later, of LINESMAN/MEDIATOR. Sir Alec was Chief Engineer of the RAF until his retirement in 1983. He is very welcome today.

Sandy Hunter asked if I would try to cover the development of the UK C&R System from the end of the war through the ROTOR programme and beyond – the beyond we agreed should not go further than the LINESMAN/MEDIATOR move to West Drayton and that is what I shall try to do.

With most large scale defence developments you start with the threat and a requirement. You then get into the finances with the Treasury but you hope not too deeply into the political arena. Finally you reach the technology, the PE and the industry and start a programme of work with its over optimism, subsequent delays and its cost over-runs. You will not be surprised that the development of the UK C&R System was quite standard in all these parameters and had a high rating in some of them.

At its full extent in May 1944 the C&R System consisted of 208 reporting and 33 GCI stations. These had been built up piecemeal into a highly efficient system which covered the whole of the UK. The situation in 1945 when the Home Chain was already being reduced in scope to provide resources for more pressing overseas radar deployments (eg Ottercops Moss had closed) is shown in Fig. 1. Basically, the reporting chain consisted of CH, CHL & CHEL stations while the control stations were mostly Type 7's with a few Type 13 and 14 radars for extra cover and some anti-jamming protection.

CH Stations were metric "floodlight" stations with the familiar separate transmitter and receiver towers.

CHL Stations were also metric but with a rotating aerial used for both transmitting and receiving.

CHEL Stations were centimetric stations based on the Naval 277 sets mounted on towers to provide low level cover.

Type 7's were metric radars giving PPI information and heights for direct fighter control and were the main radar for the widespread net of Ground Controlled Interception stations.

Type 13 and 14's were centimetric radars again based on the Naval 277 but giving PPI and heights for the GCI control positions.

The way in which the data from these radars was used reflected the way the system had evolved during the war. The raid reporting system passed its plots by voice to filter rooms, to Fighter Command, Fighter Groups, Sector Operation Rooms and to Royal Observer Corps and coastal AA Operation Rooms. Fighters were then scrambled under the control of the Sector Ops Room or occasionally by Group Ops Room and then finally handed over to GCI control for the final stages of the interceptions. Fighter aircraft positions could be monitored by triangulation on their VHF speech transmissions. Such a system, though it had been made to work well, had obvious weaknesses mainly due to errors of plotting, delays in track information and imprecise identification of enemy aircraft.

Towards the end of the war in Europe, the Air Ministry gave some thought to the shape and organisation of the post-war air defences as well as to the type of radars and data processing equipment it required. As early as July 1945 it issued a paper proposing a "Defended Area" to be manned by a regular nucleus capable of expansion at short notice and a "Shadow Area" where a non-operational air defence network would be available and be able to be fully operational in 2 years manned by a trained but non-regular reserve force. It also contemplated 600 knot targets flying at 80 to 100,000 feet which meant early warning radars with 330 miles ranges at 60,000 feet and about 200 miles at sea level. It looked for a secure IFF system and a display of the recognised air picture that could be transmitted up to 1,000 miles. Although these requirements were soundly based, the parlous financial state of the country at the end of the war dictated that little could be done.

Fighter Command worked hard to set up the Defended Area from Flamborough Head to Portland Bill (Fig 2) based on its concept of Master GCI stations but its efforts were hampered when the Government called for a rapid run down of manpower which left only 36 radars operational of which 7 were GCI's and 3 CH's. There were no people for Care and Maintenance and so most of the CHL and CHEL equipments were moved into the nearest CH stations for safety. By late '46 and early '47 the lowest point of the system was reached because of critical shortages of trained manpower, particularly radar mechanics and fitters. I can personally remember fault-finding by telephone from 73 Wing Headquarters on radar sets up and down the East Coast using mechanics on site who had no knowledge of the equipment beyond how to switch it on. As a young newly joined pilot officer I felt this was close to the blind leading the blind. Despite the difficulties Fighter Command did set up experimentally 4 Master GCI's at Sopley, Trimley Heath, Neatishead and Patrington using Type 7, Type 11 and Type 13 radars. It managed to conduct major exercises in 1948 and 49 once the Berlin Airlift had become necessary and there was again some interest in defence spending.

The Berlin Airlift and the formation of NATO eventually brought a new directive to Fighter Command in 1949 which was "the defence of the UK against air attack". Such an explicit directive obviously called for a complete review of the C&R system which was in a shaky state and the requirement was based on the work done at the end of the war calling for new radars, data processing and identification systems. It was not possible to meet these requirements in the short term and the best that could be done quickly was to up-date the old war time system by duplicating the radar cover, making some of it mobile, going underground for protection where possible, making the radars more reliable and easier to maintain and improving the readiness by deploying more manpower on watch. This was the ROTOR Programme which was part of the UK 1950 Defence Programme stimulated by the attack on South Korea from the North. Importantly the programme included a measure to call up Z Class Reserves for 15 days' training a year with 10,000 officers and men allotted to man the C&R System in an emergency.

The concept of the ROTOR plan was applied to the Defended Area immediately, it provided for radar cover of Northern England to follow as soon as possible and for the sea approaches thereafter. It allowed for 8 SOC's and included 63 radar sites in all, but always envisaged new radars would be ready for deployment in 1957 which would greatly simplify the system. The deployments in early 1954 are shown in Fig 3. Contracts were let to Marconi, Metropolitan Vickers, Cossors and BTH to modify the old war time radars but the follow-on radars were more of a problem. At one point it looked as if the C&R system might have to use the Naval 984 3D radar but in the event technological progress with radar components suddenly made the TRE Type 80 radar so promising by the end of 1951 that several were ordered and began to be installed towards the end of 1954, long before the 1957 date which had been expected. This had a great effect on the ROTOR programme.

The Type 80 was really a "horizon limited radar" able to see down to the horizon, ie, 22,000 feet at 200 nms. Such solid long range cover showed that the same radar could in future be used for reporting and control and could cut down the number of radars required and reduce the data transmission problems enormously. It also enabled a real-time photographic system of recording the air situation to be produced and used for control and later for training. By the end of 1958 the number of ROTOR stations had effectively been reduced from the 63 originally envisaged to 35.

The development of the hydrogen bomb in the West and in Russia led gradually to the adoption of the theory of deterrence and with it the short 3-day concept of war. This required that if deterrence failed, high speed, high altitude enemy aircraft carrying H bombs would have to be destroyed at all costs before reaching the UK coast. The solid overland radar cover provided by ROTOR in its early stages was not designed for this scenario and it was clear the system required major changes both in equipment and organisation.

Based on the Type 80 radars, EW and GCI could not continue as separate entities and the Fighter Command plan proposed an Integrated C&R System based on Master GCI Stations which took over many of the old SOC duties. The integrated system would be simpler, have more rapid response to air threats, give more accurate control of aircraft and be capable of controlling SAGW defences. The approaches to the UK were divided into 9 areas or sub-sectors as shown in Fig 4. Each area contained a 'comprehensive' radar – a Type 80 for control and reporting with first call on specified fighter airfields. Boulmer was chosen for trials as the first comprehensive station. The sub-sector commander was at the Type 80 station with 'raw radar' data on a photographic projection screen. He issued instructions to Chief Controllers around him and they in turn to Controllers in charge of up to 4 interception consoles.

The plan gave about 3,000 manpower savings and allowed the system to go to a 3 watch basis. This was very important since National Service came to an end in 1957 and abruptly reduced the available manpower in the C&R system. However, though the Fighter Command plan made good progress, both manpower and money problems caused the system to be reduced in size. Furthermore, there were those who thought that with ballistic missiles coming there would be little need for a C&R system and that the bombshell arrival of the French carcinotron jammer had probably made ground radars obsolete.

Initially the existence of the carcinotron was a great blow to the C&R system. It was effectively a magnetron which unlike all previous magnetrons did not just have one fixed frequency but was able to produce RF energy at various frequencies merely by the variation of one voltage applied to the device. This feature coupled with its useful power output meant an airborne jammer could attack ground radars whatever their frequency of operation. However, as with most threats it is possible to counter attack and this is what happened. A technology counter was adopted and produced the Type 85 radar and the associated Passive Detection System.

In the case of the radar it resulted in a very high power S Band radar with a big (60' x 21') aerial system, low side lobes and a most sophisticated receiver. It had 12 overlapping beams in the vertical plane, it could switch frequency from pulse to pulse and radiate up to 8 megawatts peak power to help "burn through" the carcinotron jamming signals. The Type 85 collaborated with the Passive Detection

System which was the second string in the counter to the carcinotron or any other RF jammer. This system worked by receiving jamming from an aircraft at two or more sites on the ground and comparing and correlating these signals in a special way to give a fix on the jammer aircraft and also to overcome the "ghosting" or false targets problem which occurs when more than one jammer is operating. Four PDS sites were eventually commissioned at Neatishead, Staxton, Boulmer and Dundonald and they were very effective as tested by the Canberra ECM squadron. Together these two techniques led to confidence in the C&R system returning and the preparation of PLAN AHEAD which was approved in January 1959. This plan relied on Type 85 radars and the Passive Detection System and relegated the more easily jammed Type 80 radars to a secondary role on the periphery. The plan also incorporated several Type 84 L-Band radars which were better for Moving Target Indication (MTI) and clutter rejection than the S-Band Type 85s.

The control system in use was centred on the Type 80 radar stations. Unfortunately it was not possible to use the Type 85 station in the same way because of the "zenithal gap" in the radar cover and also because there was a need for PDS information from two or more other stations. A data handling and computing system had therefore to be installed and a Master Control Centre set up taking track data from all the tracking stations. The costs of PLAN AHEAD rose quickly from £30m to £100m causing its scale to be curtailed to a minimum system of 3 radar tracking stations with PDS and one Master Control Centre.

The Master Control Centre was planned to go underground at Bawburgh but after considerable confusion which finally involved the Prime Minister (Harold Macmillan) and the Chief of the Air Staff (Sir Thomas Pike), the RRE proposal to use West Drayton as the MCC above ground was accepted. This was on condition that limited data extraction and control facilities would be available at the radar tracking stations in case the MCC at West Drayton was ever out of action. In the event, only manual facilities were allowed because of Treasury opposition to the extra expense.

This involvement of the Prime Minister in PLAN AHEAD had a fundamental effect upon the UK Air Defence System because he ruled that PLAN AHEAD should only proceed if it gave an advantage to the national Air Traffic Control Services. In effect this gave birth to LINESMAN/MEDIATOR in February 1961 and later to the

National Air Traffic Service with MATO and CATO as its military and civil elements. It also meant that the military C&R system ended up with two severe vulnerabilities in the MCC at West Drayton:

First, the above ground, unprotected building and

Secondly, to meet the civil requirement to control aircraft using raw radar data, the unprotected tower-mounted wide band radio links instead of the underground cables carrying processed data which the Royal Air Force preferred.

The diagram of the proposed LINESMAN/MEDIATOR C&R System at Fig 5 shows the complexity that was inevitable in specifying and finally commissioning such an enormous data processing project. One has to remember that it was still early days in computing and today's commonplace processors, CD Roms and virtual reality were not even gleams in the developers' eyes. Indeed, there were considerable computer programming problems and mostly there was a crisis around the corner requiring more programmers, more memory, more floor space and more time and money to complete – not to mention the swift march forward in computer technology which made the equipment obsolescent almost before it was installed.

The LINESMAN part seemed fairly straightforward from the planning angle – 3 radar stations, PDS, the MCC control for Lightnings and Bloodhound and links to the NATO system. MEDIATOR however was more difficult with 3 ATCC's, 8 airways radars, 4 ATCRU's, the introduction of secondary surveillance radars and the whole complexity of flight plan processing to deal with.

By early 1964 these difficulties led to the breakdown of the project into its constituents – LINESMAN and MEDIATOR – and, by mid 1968, Press criticism of the whole endeavour as too vulnerable and too obsolescent led to a reconsideration (the Moulton Report) and simplification of the LINESMAN portion. West Drayton became a Tactical Control Centre passing data to Strike Command Ops Centre (STCOC) and its fighter and SAGW control positions were removed to the radar stations which were then equipped with SLEWC (Standby Early Warning & Control System) to give them local fighter and SAM control. This was in fact a return to the old maxim which had proved so successful in the early C&R system – Centralised control of the air battle BUT Decentralised control of the engagements.

It also finally met the requirement to provide a local control capability at the radars which had been called for in 1961 when West

Drayton was accepted as the MCC and which the Treasury had effectively vetoed.

Several peripheral radars were replaced and extra height finders installed but eventually LINESMAN was declared complete in December 1973 – "within the timescale and £600K below the projected cost". I don't know how economical with the truth that statement was when it was made but how well the LINESMAN coverage at 30,000ft. matched the UKADR boundary in the end is shown in Fig. 6. Clearly, at lower levels there was a much less favourable match between the two but, in the North, in particular, the Shackleton AEW aircraft with its rather antiquated American radar gallantly filled some of the gaps – some of the time.

That is where my story ends. It is the story of a system evolving under all the influences which surround the development of extensive military projects – world events, political will, the state of the national economy, technological achievements, industrial competence and so on. But there is never an end to the development of a system such as the UK C&R System. As with all the previous changes that had taken place, no sooner was LINESMAN complete than Roy Austin-Smith began studying how to improve the system and his report led us inevitably into UKADGE and all the present day NATO procurement problems which fortunately I can leave for others to discuss with you.

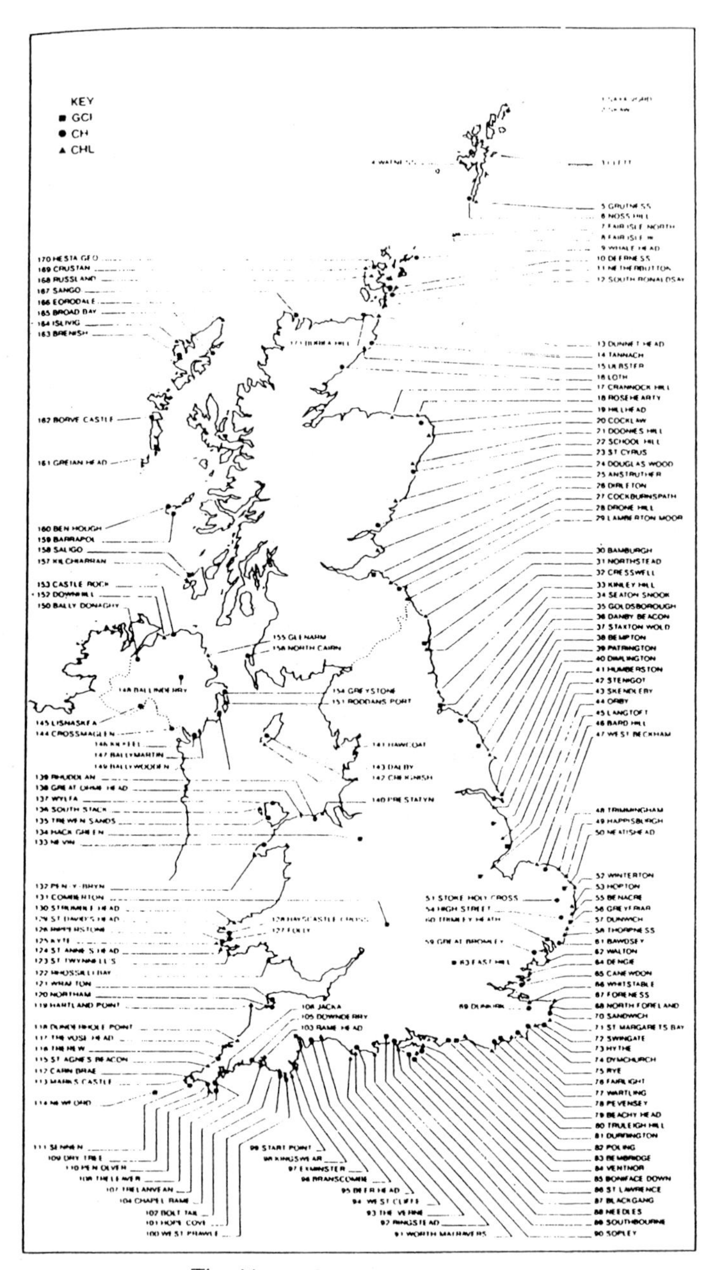

The Home Chain March 1945

Figure I

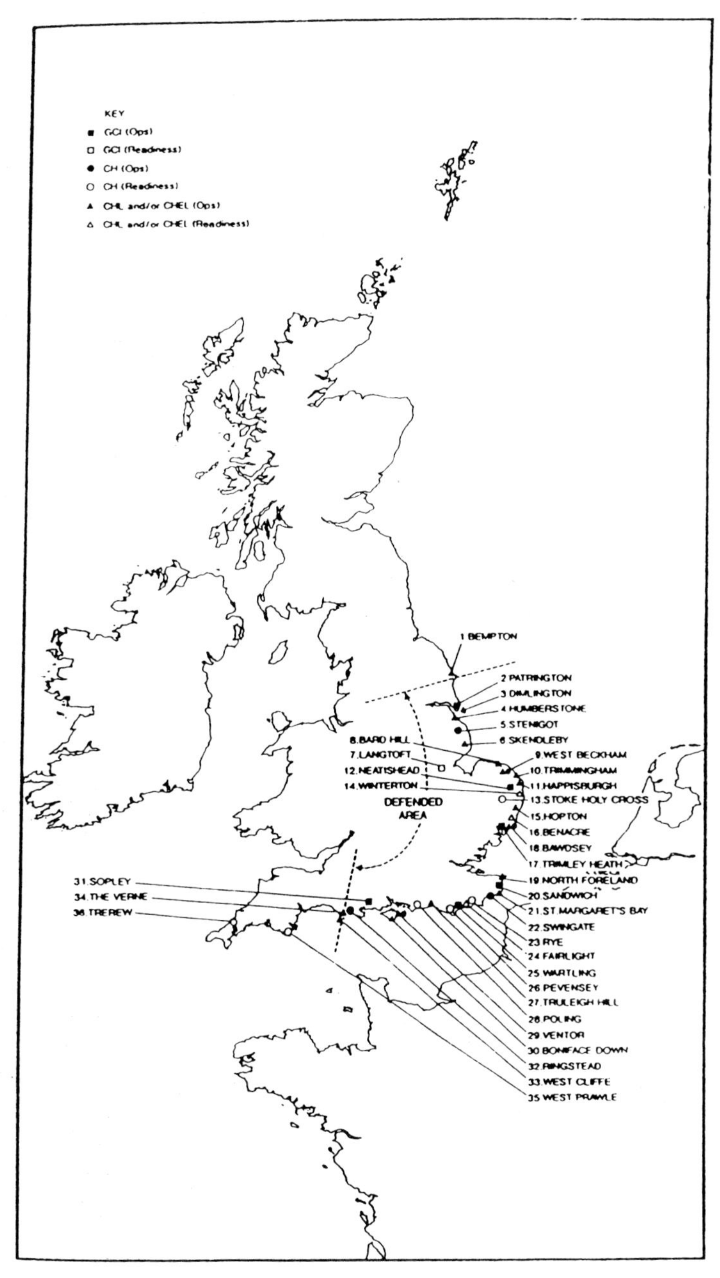

Radar Stations in 1947 : The Defended Area

Figure II

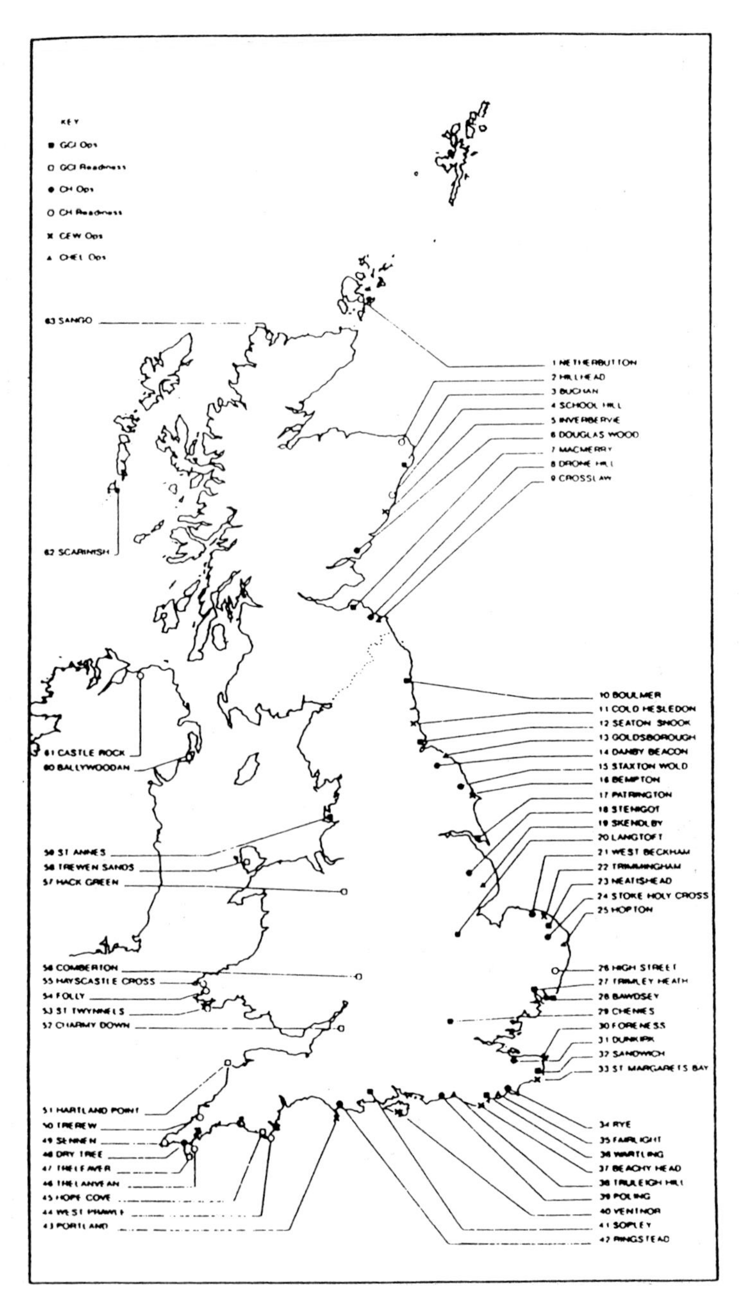

Rotor Stations Early 1954

Figure III

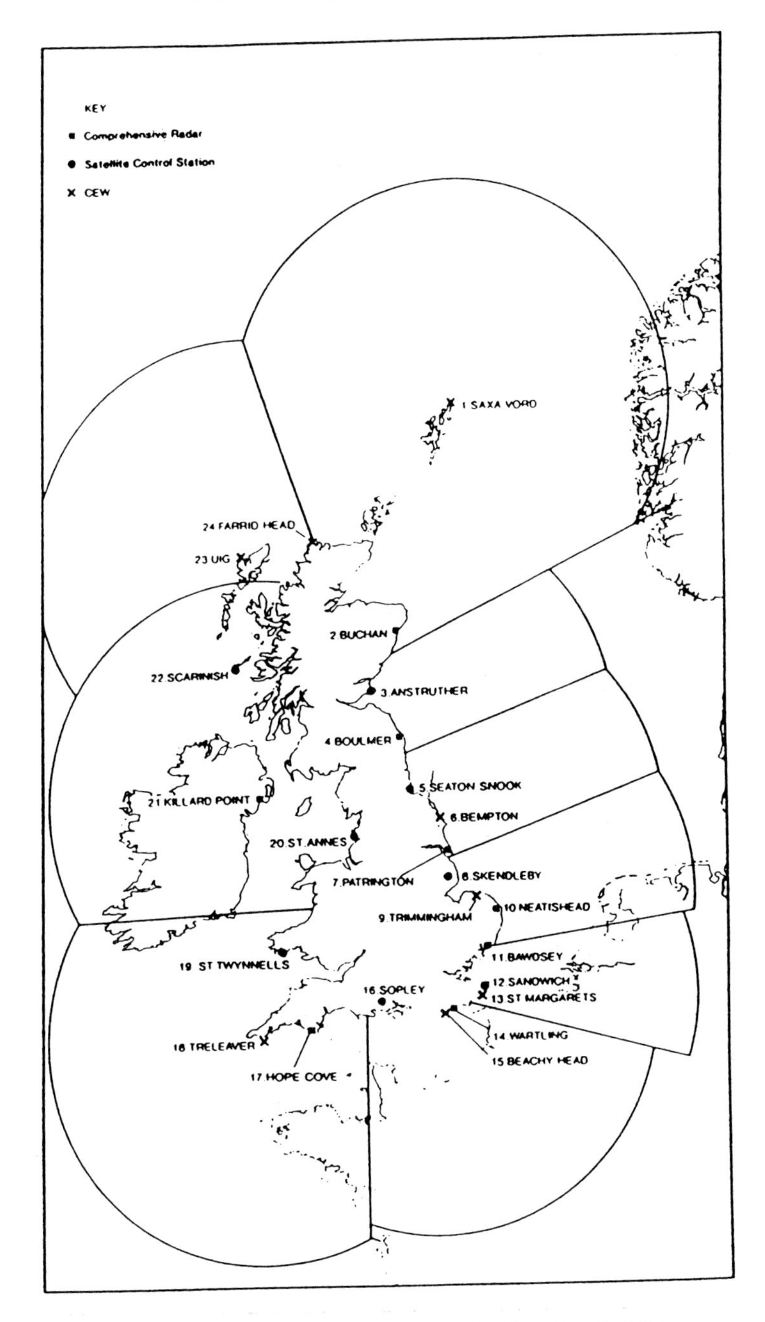

Radar Stations 1958 Signals Plan for ADUK

Figure IV

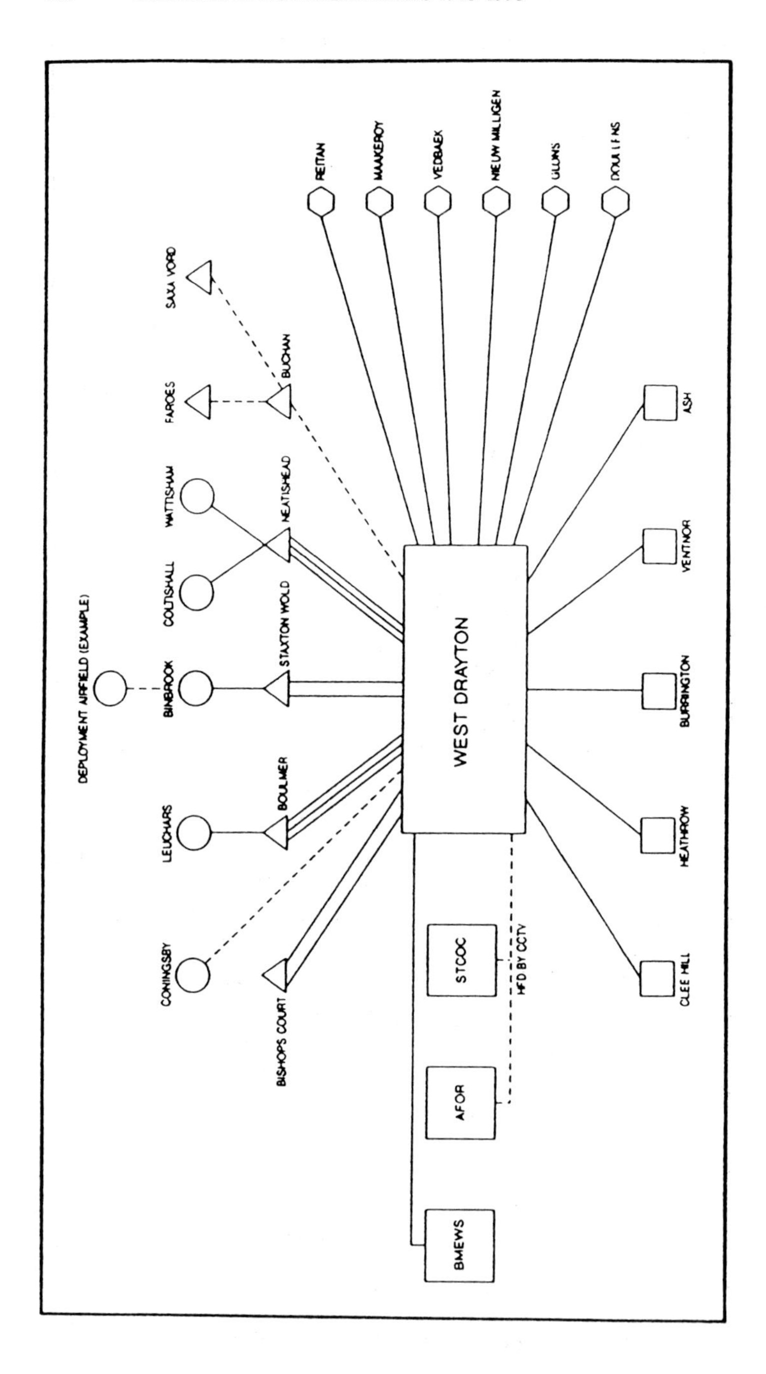

The LINESMAN MEDIATOR C & R System

Figure V

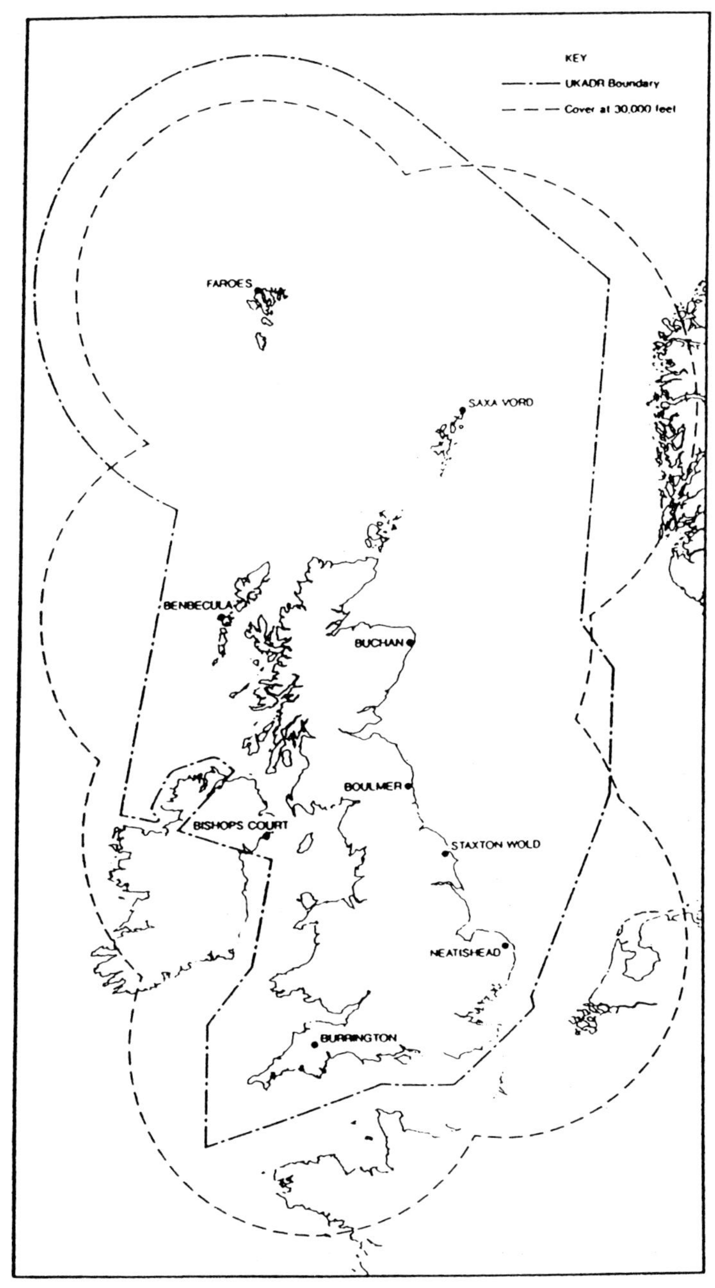

UKADR Boundary and LINESMAN 30,000 ft Cover : 1973

Figure VI

From Lightning to F4

Chairman:

The 25 years following the 50s were very much the years of two great aircraft, the Lightning and the Phantom. These saw great changes to the horizons of air defence, not least in pushing out the defensive boundaries of the entire UK.

Air Cdre Ian McBRIDE is one of my oldest friends in the RAF. He and I trained for our wings together at Acklington in the early 60s and I was able to observe his career in Air Defence from a distance as he served at Leuchars on No. 74 Sqn. and at Coltishall on the staff of the Lightning OCU. Later, he commanded No. 43 Sqn., again at Leuchars, and the RAF Germany AD Base at Wildenrath. He was later in charge of the AD branches at the Central tactics and Trials Organization and Strike Command and was Director of Air Defence in the MoD before leaving the Service.

It is a rare event indeed to be invited to talk on your chosen subject for as long as you like without any responsibility for what you say, no constraints as to how you are to approach the subject and all this without the burden of having to produce a script. It was only after I had accepted this well-baited invitation that the real requirement started to emerge, the actual rules of engagement were promulgated and the full extent of Sandy Hunter's treachery became clear. I suppose that my own gullibility might also have been a factor.

My task is to discuss the role of the Lightning and Phantom aircraft in the prosecution of UK air defence duties using RAF Leuchars as a model but with Leconfield and Middleton St. George also in mind. In theory the period covered by these two aircraft runs from the late 50s to the early 90s but in reality they only form the core of the front line between about 1964 when the Lightning finally supplanted the Javelin in the UK, and 1989 when the 3rd Tornado ADV base came on stream at RAF Leeming just down the road from here. In effect I have to cram nearly 30 years into just less than 30 minutes!

The Lightning and Phantom era saw massive change in terms of the strategic setting of the air defence task, the composition and the capability of the threat posed to the UK, and the technology available or deployed as part of our defensive array. It also saw a swing in the policy of selecting aircrew for duties on brand-new aircraft, and a quantum improvement in the realism and effectiveness of routine aircrew training. Although not an expert in the field I will also mention parallel developments in the air defence ground environment and how changes in air equipment and tactics spilled over or were reflected in this area. It was an exciting time for us all, not least because of the wholesale changes which were either forced upon us or generated internally.

Returning to the UK theme of this personal perspective, I shall deal first with the strategic backdrop to the period and discuss the implications of major change in this area in terms of the air defence posture adopted throughout the period. I shall then address how some elements of the UK air defence system developed, or otherwise, in response to changing circumstances or capabilities, and will point up a few of the command and control issues which characterised this period. Inevitably for one whose métier was the tactical employment of weapons and systems, I shall dwell a while on the strengths and weaknesses of the tools at the disposal of the air defence commanders of the day. It will be interesting to hear the extent to which things have improved over the intervening years.

The Lightning entered service against the background of a strategic nuclear posture known severally as massive nuclear retaliation or, by CND and others, as Mutually Assured Destruction. The general notion was that any military incursion by either Bloc would result in all-out nuclear exchanges with little or no involvement of conventionally armed forces. Its successor, known throughout NATO as MC 14/3 or the Strategy of Flexible Response, allowed for a graduated escalation of weapon or force employment with a threshold at which nuclear 'shots across the bow' would be employed. If these failed to deter the aggressor, an escalating sequence of tactical, theatre and then strategic nuclear exchanges would probably have followed. This shift of emphasis opened up the prospect of a coherent and therefore credible build-up of conflict, provided that this could be controlled at every level and that only a measured and proportional response was taken to any incursion or attack. It is self-evident that this strategy placed far greater emphasis on the employment of tactical, conventionally armed forces than did its predecessor.

The first was characterised by an initial salvo of long-range nuclear-tipped missiles which would have been detected by the BMEWS radars. This would have triggered a number of parallel actions within the UK and elsewhere but, in the context of this gathering, the relevant fact is that the air defence fighters would have been scrambled for survival. The effect of this vertical dispersal of vital air defence assets was that they should have been airborne at the time of arrival of the incoming warheads, and thus survived the blast and heat effects of these weapons. Whether their radios would have withstood the effects of the electromagnetic pulses associated with nuclear events is rather less likely, an eventuality of which we were all blissfully unaware at the time.

The importance of these radios becomes significant at the next stage of the procedure when the fighters would have been told which airfields were unaffected by nuclear effects and fallout, and were to be used for the next phase of air defence operations. The perception was that this would consist of mass raids by manned bombers, some of them supersonic, countered by fighters scrambled from the ground to intercept autonomously, or launched against discrete targets if local or continental early warning so allowed.

In contrast it was thought that the defensive campaign associated with the strategy of flexible response would be characterised by an initial spell of enemy surveillance missions which would also probe our defences to detect weakness and establish the vigour with which the air defence commander was prepared to prosecute his task. This period of tension and intelligence gathering would probably have been the precursor to attacks by conventionally armed missiles launched from stand-off air platforms. The classic exercise scenario of the day saw these weapons being aimed at air defence airfields and associated control centres. Follow-up attacks by manned aircraft might then have materialised, concentrating on air bases, weapon storage areas, assembly and trooping areas and other fixed sites. Received wisdom allowed attacks against nuclear storage facilities and operating bases at this juncture but not against BMEWS and the like. Such a move would have been considered at the strategic level to have been escalatory even though we at the tactical level would have considered them to have been fair game.

The tempo of events differed markedly between the 2 strategies. The first started with a bang (or more accurately a series of bangs) and then continued in an indeterminate fashion whereas the second was characterised by a long and progressive build-up, culminating in a flash or series of flashes. In the first you fought with whatever survived the initial exchange whereas in the second you had to fight through a conventional phase targeted on you in order to survive until one combatant or another initiated an all-out nuclear phase, or sued for peace.

At the risk of further over-simplifying things, the Lightning can be considered the main defensive aircraft of the first strategy and the Phantom the latter, although in reality the distinction is not that clear or straightforward. However I would like to harness this label to illustrate how each type of campaign shaped its own equipment requirements and generated a wholly different tactical employment of air defence assets.

Let me now address a range of operational issues in an attempt to paint a picture of the era and indicate how each aircraft meshed with its environment and drove the tactical thinking of its day. As I have already said, these were exciting times and many new capabilities were being introduced. These in turn spawned new tactics and doctrine, these often required revisions to the training system, and so on. It was a continuous process in which, sadly, some good things fell by the wayside and some hard-won lessons had to be relearned.

At this early stage it is worth mentioning the mechanisms available for the introduction of change because these had a great bearing on the extent and, more importantly, the rate at which change was implemented.

The arrival of the Lightning in service coincided, to all intents and purposes, with the demise of the Central Fighter Establishment (or CFE) which had reigned supreme in terms of tactical doctrine and weapon employment for earlier aircraft. CFE played an important part in setting things up for the Lightning but its status was soon changed and its lineal descendant was little more than a trials unit. The net result was that for a significant period in the development of the Lightning as a fighting machine there was no central co-ordinating and guiding agency with the muscle to force things through. Seminars were held and many ideas aired, but because the work of implementing them fell to hard-pressed staff officers with other agendas and priorities, many of these ideas never saw the light of day.

Fortunately for all concerned this state of affairs was reversed towards the end of the 60s with the formation of the Central Tactics and Trials Organisation, a unit established, resourced and mandated to ensure that doctrine, tactics, trials and equipments were all coherently linked in a timely and user-friendly fashion. This important outfit cut its teeth on the Lightning but really made its mark with the Phantom. There is no doubt that the CTTO played a massively important part in keeping the front-line up to speed with changes in doctrine, many of which were prompted by that other child of the late 60s, the dreaded TACEVAL. I do not intend to spend the rest of the session describing this institution but will confine myself to saying that whilst it demanded full compliance with – and adherence to – NATO and national procedures, and was undoubtedly a force for good, it also wrecked some promising careers and cast a long shadow over life in the fun-loving peacetime air force that was being projected in the advertisements of the day. I doubt if anybody seriously doubts the value of TACEVAL and the positive influence that it had on the way that we did business, but there were times when the wrong lessons were drawn from its results.

What I would like to do now is to take a brief look at the way that the air defence task was done before and after the advent of 14/3 and attempt to put some figures of merit on how well we did. After several stabs at this section, each finishing up as a longer, more rambling and brain-numbing dirge than its predecessor, I sought solace in the old ATP33 whose chapters were of course the staff of life for so many of the warriors here today. This authoritative and utterly forgettable document breaks the air defence process down into components which we can examine in turn.

- Detection
- Identification
- Classification
- Passage of Information

- Assignment of Weapon System
- Control of Weapons
- Recovery of System

Detection, Identification and Classification

In the era of the Big Bang strategy the first offensive raid was always assumed to be a long-range missile strike, and few of us reckoned that this would pass unnoticed. The BMEWS would detect these missiles early enough to allow a survival scramble from which air defence and V-force aircraft would recover to home or pre-ordained bases to set up for the next phase. There were moves late in the life of this strategy to minimise the warning available from BMEWS by using low trajectory non-ballistic profiles but these were not developed in time to feature in this era. It is all pure conjecture of course, but if these re-shaped profiles had materialised they might have had a significant effect on our ability to survive and thus our subsequent combat posture. On the other hand, the Lightning with its unsurpassed ability to get airborne in a hurry, was unlikely to get caught on the ground in this way. The Phantom, also no slouch on its day, was however rather more likely to have had a close encounter with incoming weapons.

Detection of incoming raids in the 14/3 era was a different matter altogether. The initial threat was generally perceived to consist of probing sorties by recce or armed attack aircraft in a phase which would have tested our comms and rules of engagement in a big way. The received wisdom is that these would have been followed by attacks using long-range stand-off missiles, aimed at the control and reporting organisation in the first instance. The aim of these was to poke our eyes out and give us a massive problem detecting the follow-up attacks. In later years these sites were hardened or given redundancy by equipping them with mobile radars in addition to their fixed arrays. During the era under consideration little reliance could be placed upon UK land-based radars for detection of attacks although the links and procedures for continental early warning were coming on line. Nor could the fighters contribute much in the early days. The endurance of the Lightning was such that it was called upon to cruise around at the tropopause where its chances of autonomously detecting an incoming bomber were poor at the best of times and just about zero if the raider were to approach at less than 30,000 feet. In the fullness of time it was recognised that the Lightning had a very reasonable chance of a radar detection on a target if the antenna was pointed upwards, away from the heavy ground clutter which undermined its pulse radar performance. This had the added advantage of exploiting the aircraft's quite extraordinary climb performance and also allowing it to approach a target from well within its blind spot, thereby enhancing the kill potential of the Lightning's barely adequate weapon system. Any loss in 'on-task' endurance incurred by this form of tactical employment was more than offset by the burgeoning use of air-to-air refuelling to keep aircraft airborne on productive combat air patrols for as long as crew bladders and weapon states allowed. The tactical employment of AAR on air defence operations was probably the single greatest step forward of the era insofar as the fighters were concerned. It had a profound effect on their effectiveness and greatly eased the management of resource. No longer was it necessary to scramble fighter aircraft against short-range pickups by land-based radars, often with disappointing results, or keep Combat Air Patrol or CAP stations manned at great expense in terms of fighter availability for other tasks. AAR allowed fighters to hold an airborne alert state for relatively long periods, giving the Air Defence Commander the opportunity to hit incoming targets early and also allowing him to hold fewer of his aircraft at high readiness on the ground, a defensive posture which could be very debilitating in terms of sustainability. There has been a lot of debate over the years as to how we should define the role of AAR in support of ADOPS. Various terms have been used, including 'Force Multiplier', 'Force Extender', and 'Force Enabler'. The Treasury liked 'Force Multiplier' because it allowed them to divide the funds allocated to UK Air Defence in proportion to the multiplication factor! In truth all the terms are equally applicable and any could be used to describe the crucial role played by AAR. It goes without saying that the increase in UK Air Defence effectiveness which resulted from its introduction was immediate and dramatic.

The other major improvement in our air defence posture was rather slower to appear on the scene in RAF colours but, after a tentative start, it came on line in time to combine very effectively with both the Lightning and Phantom. I refer of course to Airborne Early Warning to which I will return in a moment. Before doing so I thought that it might be useful to discuss, under the generic heading of detection which I am still (believe it or not!) addressing, to take a brief look at the detection capabilities of the two fighter aircraft of the era. The Lightning had an airborne intercept radar that was designed for use in the terminal phase of a ground-controlled interception. It was not a bad piece of kit at the time of its introduction but the range at which a target could be seen on this basic pulse radar could not be described as anything more than modest at high level and very much less in the high clutter environment at 5,000 feet and below over the sea. I am not trying to denigrate the radar or its operators; quite the reverse. They produced results which bordered on amazing but they were working with equipment which was designed in another age and for a different concept of operations. It is also interesting to observe that the radar performance of the 2-seat aircraft was often better than that attained by the 1-man crew, especially at low level and/or at night. The young tearaway with his hair on fire might not agree with this observation but the cooler, wiser head in the audience might reluctantly concede the point. By way of contrast, the Phantom had a truly remarkable radar (when it worked) which was capable of low-clutter detections in excess of 200 miles and low-level detections of more than 75 miles, depending on relative and absolute heights of the fighter and target. This radar gave the fighter a genuine autonomous detection capability and allowed the interception of targets as yet unseen by the ground environment, thus posing a potential Rules of Engagement problem for the Air Defence Commander. This became a greater problem in the post MC 14/3 era because the last thing that the crisis managers needed was the escalation of any conflict because some young ace had 'smoked' an unfriendly aircraft before it or any others had committed a hostile act. More on that theme later.

As I have already said, the advent of Airborne Early Warning was to revolutionise air defence. Not only did it provide target detection at all height levels at great range, thus allowing the interception of stand-off weapon carriers by CAP aircraft or the engagement of 'free-fallers' by fighters held on ground alert, but it also gave the Air Defence Commander a forward tactical control centre to which battle management decisions could be delegated or, more usually, from which battle information could be gleaned. The Lightning/Phantom era saw the AEW task being performed in turn and with varying degrees of success by Royal Navy Gannets, USAF Super Constellations, RAF Shackletons, US Navy Trackers and E-2s, RAF Nimrod Mk3's for a very short time, and finally USAF E-3 Sentries. In the fullness of time the RAF E-3D came along too but that event lies well to the right of my patch and I leave it for others to address. The only major point which I would like to make on AEW in the

Lightning and Phantom era is that this was when the UK learned the job and, although we lagged in terms of technology, we were able to show the way to the rest of the world in terms of operational proficiency and ingenuity. A number of RAF officers served with the RN on the embarked Gannet squadron and subsequently formed the nucleus of No. 8 Squadron when it re-equipped with the Shackleton. Although this aircraft lacked glamour, performance, system sophistication and a raft of other desirable qualities, its crews earned the RAF a reputation for professionalism in this field and set the standard for the rest. One always expressed relief when the ANYFACE callsign was heard on a long-range maritime or QRA task, not least because of the ability of AEW crews to establish communications with controlling authorities when all other means had seemingly failed. The meteoric rise and fall of the Nimrod AEW also occurred during this era but I do not intend to dwell on the selection of this aircraft for any longer than I already have.

For completeness I should round off this somewhat technical section with a few words on identification, a very necessary part of the air defence process which can be achieved by visual, passive electronic, active electronic or electro-optical means. The Lightning relied solely on visual identification which by day was limited by range and weather, and was difficult to achieve at all by night. However its identification capability was a better match with its weapons than was the case with the Phantom. This aircraft carried an arsenal of weapons including the AIM-7 Sparrow, replaced in due course by the UK variant, Skyflash. Both these missiles were capable of engaging targets at ranges well in excess of 12 miles, at which distance the identification of a target without recourse to some form of enhancement was well nigh impossible. The Phantom entered full RAF service in the air defence role without any aid to visual identification although US variants had carried an electro-optical device for this purpose for some time. Over the course of time it was fitted with air-to-air IFF, ESM (radar warning) and a telescope system, and its crews could carry and operate night image intensifiers of varying capability. By the time that it was retired from service the Phantom could boast a modest identification capability, albeit largely based upon a combination of methods along with an assessment of target behaviour. For their part the ADGE and the AEW Shackletons had to rely on track origin and behaviour, backed up by IFF, for identification and classification – unless they received an authenticated description from another source. I have devoted a few moments to this issue because, as weapons improved and the battleground moved further away from our fixed command and control network, so our inability to identify and classify contacts in time to use those weapons was progressively undermined.

Passage of Information

This leads me neatly on to the next issue that I wish to address, namely the passage of information around the air defence community. This requirement could range from the relatively trivial such as time checks or base weather to changes in alert states and rules of engagement or, ultimately, fall-out states. Much of this could be readily passed by telebrief to air bases and aircraft on the ground but ground-to-air communications were never entirely satisfactory. The increasing involvement of RAF fighters in the defence of maritime units increased the complexity of the communications task, and the range over which these links had to be established and maintained. For the most part the medium was the spoken word although it had always been the intention that the Lightning be equipped with a data link for the passage of data from a ground-based computer to the aircraft's auto-attack system. US and Soviet aircraft of the era were so equipped but the UK variant was never fielded.

The complexity of the communications task was immense. And it must be added that none of the links were ECM resistant or secure. It is hardly surprising therefore that there were times when about 50% of the players were working on their wits, and that the occasional 'blue-on-blue' incident resulted or ROE breach occurred during exercises. Faced with this very obvious problem the front-line operators devoted a lot of time to the development and practice of limited comms or no-radio procedures, but the bottom line is that this was a problem area which, despite considerable effort, ingenuity and training, stubbornly defied resolution.

Assignment and Control of Weapons

In the early days of the Lightning it was relatively easy for the air defence commander and his crews to assign and control the release of weapons, and thus the tempo and nature of their battle, because the overture was a massive nuclear attack which would have focused everybody's attention. Rules of engagement were relatively straightforward and the only challenge was to ensure that friendly targets were not engaged. With the rear-sector Firestreak targets would have been well within visual range throughout the final phase of the attack, provided of course that it was day/VFR at the time. Were this not the case, the relatively low closure speeds associated with these profiles would have afforded time, and thus a reasonable opportunity, to remove many residual doubts as to the classification of the target. In an era of relatively short range weapons the onus of this responsibility was not burdensome, and the likelihood of inadvertent escalation if somebody got it wrong was correspondingly low.

In the Phantom era things changed dramatically and the need to follow tautening rules of engagement was an essential part of crisis management because the price of inadvertent or premature escalation could have been very high, if not unaffordable. This dramatic shift in consequence stemmed largely from the arrival of 14/3 and the implications of that strategy but was heightened by the impressive array of weapons carried by the Phantom, and their performance. For the first time we now had in the Sparrow/Skyflash class of missile a weapon with a genuine 'beyond visual range' capability which raised a whole raft of identification, classification and tactical issues which could only be solved by tight procedural control and realistic training. That was not the end of the story because the far from adequate communications, to which I have already referred, made the control of weapons more difficult than it should have been, and our inability to ensure co-ordination of different types of weapon system made it necessary to devote certain weapons to certain geographic areas, and impose taboos on others being employed in these areas. This was all achieved and usually worked satisfactorily under exercise conditions. Whether it would have been such a success in the fog of war is another matter altogether. That said, this procedural separation undermined one of the basic tenets of air defence, namely the flexible, complementary and overlapping employment of assets, and was (I understand) only implemented with great reluctance. Nevertheless it was a problem which only arose when there were other weapon systems or aircraft to employ, and this was not always the case. When the Lightning entered service there were Bloodhound sites located in the region of V-Force bases, and the coverage of these competent systems had an impact on the areas in which Lightnings could terminate attacks. The Bloodhound disappeared from the UK scene for several years before being replaced by the Rapier. The need to integrate this weapon with fighters was relatively simple because of its inherently short range but the problem increased with the re-deployment of the Bloodhound, its job done in Germany. Throughout this period Hunters and Hawks with a peacetime training role would have augmented the front line. The original intent was to use these aircraft on CAPs near High Value targets such as air bases or ADGE sites. When these aircraft were only gun-armed the weapon control problem was of a low order but, when the Hawk was equipped with the Sidewinder, a problem of target identification and classification arose, with the imposition of dedicated engagement zones the only practical solution. When the concept of a mixed fighter force entered the frame, with radar equipped aircraft carrying out the identification on behalf of the less capable aircraft, the problem was once again contained but only to a large extent because of the skill and ingenuity of our front-line crews.

Recovery of the System

The last of the ATP33 topics that I intend to address is entitled Recovery of the System, a handle which does not fully describe the issues that I wish to raise. One of the prime requirements of any post-14/3 air defence system is resilience, or the ability to bounce back after it has been attacked and we saw this emerging as a dominant factor in the Phantom era. The perception was that the enemy would attempt to soften up defences as a major part of his initial offensive campaign, and that we, in turn, would harden our defences so as to frustrate this objective. At this juncture it has to be said that enemy attacks were considered to be all-arm and to involve a significant effort expended on incursions by groups of special forces or local terrorists. Depending on the level of threat and the relative importance of the asset that we wished to protect, our defence force might consist of RAF Regiment Rapier or Field squadrons or, at the other end of the scale, airmen diverted from their peace or war tasks to hold the line against intruders. Clearly a professional force is much more likely to provide a credible defence – and the RAF Regiment were excellent in this regard – whereas a locally raised militia was less likely to succeed whilst their absence from their established tasks would undermine our resilience elsewhere. We were well served by these lads, one of whom could be a steward and the other a clerk in the General Office, all wearing Nuclear, Biological and Chemical (NBC) defence equipment, a theme I will return to later.

As I mentioned earlier the perceived threat of the 14/3 era postulated conventional counter-air attacks on air bases with the implied intent of denying their use to our forces. It was thought that this could consist of either 'locking-in' by preventing take-offs or by locking us out by preventing landings. Although a high level of protection and redundancy was designed into our airfields, a massive engineering effort was required to restore operating surfaces in the event of them being attacked. This task fell to the Royal Engineers who had taken over the role of the long-defunct Airfield Construction Branch of the Royal Air Force.

Given the availability of an operating strip and, despite the best efforts of fighter and tanker crews, there is a finite limit to the time that can be spent in the air, even after chemical or nuclear attack. I have made passing mention of the requirement to be able to fight through the after effects of these types of attack, a posture known as Survive to Operate (STO). This posed a range of challenges including the unforgettable experience of wearing NBC kit throughout a period of intense activity. To describe this as physically debilitating, psychologically stressful and thoroughly unpleasant would probably strike a chord with anybody who has been through it. The addition of an aircrew NBC flight assembly offered the potential to fly and to fight through the effects of these dreadful weapons on recovery, during turnround, or through the subsequent launch sequence. Many of us have been asked to wear some fairly unpleasant and uncomfortable equipment in our time but I can assure those not familiar with the joys of the AR-5 aircrew NBC kit, that it takes some beating. Although it was deemed to be very effective protective equipment, the physiological stress of wearing this kit for prolonged periods would have been an unwelcome addition to the challenges already confronting our crews during a period of crisis. It follows, I believe, that the decision to adopt a defensive posture which called for the use of this equipment, rather than sit out that period in a protective shelter, would probably have been the most difficult to confront an air defence commander in the time of war.

Well there it is. I have finally raised and addressed all the issues that I felt worthy of mention in my attempt to portray our ability to perform our operational tasks during the days of the Lightning and the Phantom. There were a number of recurring themes, some of which are difficult to treat fully in open forum. There is one which I believe is central to air operations at any time and in any theatre and that is the need for realistic training, properly resourced and controlled. In the main the system and the commanders who worked within it were able to draft and implement realistic training syllabi, backed either by good synthetic training or ingeniously created scenarios, both of which sought to raise the level of our game. All too often, however, we merely managed to achieve the level which we could have used as a baseline had we been properly equipped or resourced in the first place. However one of the harshest facts of life is that the funding of air forces in peacetime always seems to fall far short of the levels demanded by the front line, whose enthusiasm, professionalism and ingenuity are often their worst enemy. This was certainly true of the period that I was asked to consider, and historians will probably, rightly or wrongly, conclude that the level of funding was adequate to win the Cold War, which (of course) we did. Perhaps we should close the book with that thought, and the memory of a proud and happy era dominated by two memorable fighting machines.

Syndicate Discussions

The Society places great stress on creating the opportunity for voices to be heard, other than those of the distinguished contributors to its seminars. In Defending Northern Skies, three discussion groups were held. The first allowed a deeper consideration of Sensors and Systems, looking at radar and other sensors, and at the command and control systems which made use of their information.

SENSORS AND SYSTEMS

Gp Capt Willbond introduced the discussion of Sensors and Systems by speaking of the continuity of principle and technique running through air defence from the first rudimentary systems of WWI. **Mr Ernest Sockett** said that he had made a detailed study of the Stockton on Tees Wireless Station and of the sound mirrors still to be seen on the North East coast. He described how information collected by the Stockton on Tees Wireless Station which intercepted transmissions from Zeppelins in flight would be fed into a warning system as early as 1914. Such information, often first obtained from transmissions as Zeppelins left Nordholz in Germany, would be fed upwards by telephone, to Rooms 40 and 49 in the Admiralty and, in the North East Region, to an Intelligence cell at No. 9 Osborne Terrace, Newcastle upon Tyne. Garrison Commanders and local telephone exchanges would be alerted and a codeword would allow the plotting of the raider's position on gridded Admiralty charts. On receipt of the word, a first warning would be passed from door to door: 'They're coming!' One target studied by Mr Sockett was the Skinningrove Iron Works near Loftus in North Yorks which, besides producing iron was, for a time, the sole supplier of mustard gas to the Army. A second or 'close' alert was obtained by the sound mirrors laid out along the coast from 1916, four of which are known to survive. Mr Sockett said the information obtained by this method was used to alert AA guns and other elements of the air defences, besides wardens who saw civilians to their shelters. Even as early as WWI, therefore, a system of detection, location, reporting and warning had been created. **Gp Capt Willbond** summed up the WWI technology and concepts from which were developed the Dowding and later air defence systems. The principles remained valid in the 1990s.

Gp Capt Colwill introduced the question of links with strategic intelligence sources which may have been a factor in WWII when deciding the deployment of air defence assets. In his experience of the Lightning days, he could not recall any such obvious linkage. **Derek Wood** observed that the suggestion that ULTRA won the Battle of Britain was balderdash! Its exploitation was in its infancy in 1940 and only a small amount of its product was usable for tactical purposes. By contrast, the product of the Y Service was much better. He agreed that the need to limit access was a factor, to the point of annoyance on the part of AOC 12 Group who was excluded from the circle. **AVM Betts** recalled that a single intelligence input existed in the sector operations rooms of 1941, no doubt to ensure careful collation and to protect sensitive sources.

AVM Betts moved on from the Stockton Wireless Station of WWI, to the great Cold War installation of Fylingdales which was part of the first billion dollar defence contract, in the USA in 1959, by which RCA set up the BMEWS chain. Sited inland to minimise the risk of seaward jamming, the first Fylingdales radar operated for over 30 years from September 1963, with a downtime of only 14 hours. Its phased array successor, capable of tracking 8,000 targets to its 800, is the most modern equipment of its kind in the world. It is certainly the biggest installation in the Defence of Northern Skies today and perhaps the most vulnerable to enemy attack. The MoD project manager for its upgrading (who was present at the seminar) recalled a suggestion current at the time that a virgin should be sacrificed upon its distinctive pyramid structure to propitiate the gods!

Sir Alec Morris was reminded that in 1944 CH radars were used in an attempt to locate the launching sites of V2 rockets. This involved a photographic device which recorded an amended timebase on which a 'streak' was displayed. A great deal of computation was needed in order to extrapolate the trajectory back to the launch point. He had come across this use of the Chain in his first posting to West Beckham CH station in Norfolk which also had the distinction of being the first to employ sealed transmitter valves, a great leap forward in technology. It was pointed out that the search for ways of using modern air defence radars to detect and track tactical missiles is a matter of current concern today.

The many offshoots of early ground radar development were mentioned, as was the success of the Royal Artillery AA defences which quickly embraced radar technology for gun and searchlight laying purposes. **Ian Brown** commented on other parallel developments, noting that the early CHL radars emerged from coastal defence surface surveillance technology developed for the Army in the first instance.

There was some discussion of the early moves to combine functions so as to create what would later become master radar stations. **Gp Capt Willbond** recalled the radar station at Northstead in Northumberland where, with the closure of Ottercops Moss in 1944 – and driven mainly by the need to save manpower – the functions of GCI and early warning radar were combined as a sort of first generation master radar station. **Sir Alec Morris** remembered how this trend continued and recalled working on a data link from Bawdsey in 1946, to send CHEL and processed CHL data to Trimley Heath as a 'comprehensive' radar station. This was but one of several experiments of that sort at the time, due according to Sir Alec, to the 'dumping' of large quantities of CHL and CHEL equipment onto the CH stations, right from the end of the war.

In a final reference to the building of the Dowding system, **Gp Capt Willbond** singled out the contribution of Sir Raymond Hart who, as a younger officer, was instrumental in the setting up of training schemes, who played a key part in developing the filter room concept and who did so much to prepare mobile radars for the Invasion. The depth of Lord Dowding's understanding and experience was constantly stressed. Derek Wood noted his ability to select and employ those capable of understanding the technologies and concepts involved in creating his great system, all at a time when there were few officers of such capacity or inclination.

The second discussion group looked at the years of World War II in the North, at the developments during that period within Fighter Command and the Air Defence of Great Britain.

FIGHTER COMMAND AND THE AIR DEFENCE OF GREAT BRITAIN

AVM Sandy Hunter introduced the discussion by reflecting on the contributions made by the Auxiliary Air Force (AAF) in WWII to the defence of Northern Skies. He spoke also of the part played by the training organisations located in the North which included such units as the No. 54 OTU at Charterhall and Winfield where urgently needed night fighter crews were trained. The unit is, perhaps, best remembered for the death in a Blenheim accident, of Richard Hillary. He was especially interested in the contribution to victory made later in the war by the setting up of the Fighter Leader School at Milfield, where the techniques and tactics of fighter ground attack were explored prior to the D Day landings.

Air Cdre Graham Pitchfork commented on the achievements of the squadrons of the AAF which too few people have recognised. The North of the UK was especially blessed by the quality and achievements of the squadrons raised there. On 15 August 1940, aircraft from bases as far apart as the Forth and the Humber, were scrambled on the instructions of HQ 13 Gp at Kenton Bar to repel a massive attack from Norway and Denmark. The part played by 616 Sqn in that battle was considerable, as was that of 607 Sqn further North. Graham Pitchfork also alluded to the evidence of the AAF's part in the Battle of Britain to be seen on the memorial panels in St. George's Chapel at Biggin Hill. There could be no doubt of the contribution and sacrifice of the AAF and its Northern squadrons.

Wg Cdr Joe Kayll had been a flight commander on No. 607 Sqn at the outbreak of war and one of its original Auxiliary members. He said that there had really been no great urgency in the months leading up to the war when, perhaps, only a little more training had been undertaken. The Squadron was then equipped with the Gladiator, a marvellous aerobatic aircraft but of a very dated design. After a false start when the squadron had been mobilised but then stood down, it was 'embodied' into the RAF in August 1939. Shortly afterwards, it was moved to Acklington ('to be nearer Scotland' – and the Forth anchorages) and the second or third aircraft to be shot down fell to the guns of Flt Lt John Sample and Fg Off Dudley Craig. The very articulate Luftwaffe pilot of the Do18 destroyed by them commented that 'to be shot down by a bloody barrister in a bloody biplane is more than I can bloody well bear'! The squadron moved to France with its Gladiators and only later was it re-equipped 'because (the RAF) did not want to spare Spitfires and Hurricanes – and quite right too!' On arrival in France, flying ceased for lack of spares and only by some ingenuity did the Auxiliaries contrive to get airborne, generally on the pretext of airtesting.

Asked about experience levels at the outbreak of war, **Wg Cdr Kayll** said that he had had nearly 1,000 hours but had been one of the Squadron's earliest pilots: most had much less than that and a few had to be left behind who were not fully trained. Training was 'really pretty minimal' and consisted of a fortnight's camp and weekends. However, it was the sheer enthusiasm of the Auxiliaries that made the Squadron what it was. In the regular cadre, besides two officer flying instructors, two or three tradesmen SNCOs and perhaps ten airmen looked after the aircraft and trained the auxiliary groundcrew. These were often skilled workers from the shipyards, the mines and the factories.

A number of matters concerning radar in WWII were raised and it was noted by more than one speaker how effectively secrecy was maintained. Although pilots on 607 Squadron knew, for example, of the existence of Ottercops Moss CH station, they had no access to it or liaison with its staff. In the same way, **Mrs Sainsbury** pointed out that, even in the HQ 13 Gp Operations Room, there was no detailed knowledge of how the information coming from the RDF stations was obtained. It was a different part of the Air Force and that was that.

The difficulties of weather facing attackers and defenders operating over the inhospitable North Sea were highlighted by **Dr Vincent Orange.** Range was not a problem for the Luftwaffe who could attack from Norway or Denmark and reach most places in the British Isles, often with the advantage of sophisticated navigation and bombing aids. Glasgow was well within reach and the West of the country could be threatened from the Brest and Cotentin peninsulas, an approach which made navigation somewhat easier against coastal targets. That said, **Sebastian Cox** recalled the bombing of Dublin, mistaken for Belfast, and reminded those present of the navigational difficulties presented by wartime conditions. The combination of North Sea weather, pitch darkness, minimal training and primitive aircraft and navigation aids, caused at least one speaker to marvel at how it was that aircraft managed to return to the ground successfully, let alone carrying out any offensive or defensive task. **Wg Cdr Kayll** stressed the experience gained by members of the AAF whose pre-war flying had constantly stressed the navigational skills, map reading and meticulous pre-flight planning. But the fact remained that large navigational errors were common: the example was quoted of a flight of Hampdens making a landfall in the Firth of Forth, rather than the Moray Firth – and then being shot down by the defending Spitfires of No. 602 Sqn. from Drem whose marksmanship was better than their aircraft recognition.

The part played by weather in the death of Richard Hillary when under training as a night fighter pilot at Charterhall was mentioned by **Capt Sainsbury.** He suggest that the allocation of 'clapped out' aircraft to OTUs and the posting as OTU instructors of unwilling and untrained aircrew, were probable factors in the death of Hillary and the many others who perished. He refuted any notion of a suicide. Charterhall was, by many accounts, not a popular or happy station but the pressure to produce crews was probably irresistible. By contrast, Milfield was described to **Vincent Orange** by the New Zealand fighter pilot, Johnny Checketts, as having provided a very valuable training at the Fighter Leaders School. There the techniques of ground attack were taught under the guiding influence of the then Gp Capt Batchy Atcherley who was on the training staff at HQ AEAF. **Capt Sainsbury** noted that, to this day, work continues to remove unexploded ordnance from Goswick Sands, the location of Atcherley's great air to ground range.

In summing up, **Sandy Hunter** reflected that the squadrons and stations of the North had played an important part in the air defence of the British Isles. The rapid extension of the Dowding system to the North, notably to cover the anchorages at Scapa Flow and the Forth had made possible the successes achieved by day against attack from Scandinavia. The notable events of 15 August 1940 served, as was pointed out by Sir Robert Watson-Watt in an interview after the War, as a perfect example of the workings of the System. Those involved in every aspect of the Defence of Northern Skies thus earned a place in the history of the Battle of Britain itself. Later, less intensive action by the night defences had ensured the relative safety of the important industrial areas of the North.

The final discussion group was especially lively and brought out a wealth of previously 'lost' material and information about Post War Developments.

POST WAR DEVELOPMENTS

Gp Capt Ian Madelin began by reflecting that air defence is probably the least studied and written about aspect of RAF operations since WWII. Accordingly Defending Northern Skies presented an opportunity for many of those attending to make a contribution to the recorded history of the Service.

Opening a discussion on the RAuxAF, **Bill Beaumont** said that he had commanded No. 3609 (West Riding) Sqn which had had various roles, including the dispatch of a mobile radar to Tiree and the provision of a fourth watch at Shipton, the Sector Operations Centre of the Northern Sector. At weekends it manned Patrington and Bempton, a commitment shared with the East Riding unit based at Hull. Until the arrival of the Type 80 radar, these units made up for shortages in regular manpower and included well qualified people such as Post Office and TV engineers, besides ex National Servicemen. He judged that they were in many ways at least as well trained and experienced as their regular counterparts.

Air Cdre Ian Atkinson spoke of his time as Adjutant of 613 (City of Manchester) Sqn which had a wartime operating base at Thornaby and, at its home base at Ringway, was part of an all-Auxiliary force in Western Sector. He noted that nearly all the squadron's tradesmen were employed in the aircraft industry, a source of manpower not existing to the same extent today. **Robert Jackson** recalled that Auxiliary pilots had successfully flown the Hunter prior to disbandment of the RAuxAF, a fact noted in the ORBs of regular Hunter squadrons. That, and the experience of other countries, lent the lie to suggestions that reservists could not cope with aircraft more advanced than the Vampire and Meteor.

The cost of equipping Auxiliary squadrons with more modern aircraft was argued by **Ian Madelin** to be at the heart of the decision to disband the flying squadrons of the RAuxAF, not proficiency in the air, although **Bill Beaumont** stressed that the manpower costs were trivial. **Air Cdre Ian McBride** said that, as a front line squadron and station commander in the 80s, he was hard pressed to sustain 24 hour air defence operations, because of peacetime manning levels. He believed that individual reservists, rather than formed units, could have been brought up to speed by careful training in a build up period. He recalled that attempts in other roles to trial such a scheme had foundered on the rocks of a hostile and negative attitude on the part of the regulars. **Air Cdre Dennis Caldwell** suggested that it would have been hard to provide sufficient flying hours for a reservist cadre but **Ian McBride** said that he believed that the experiment had been thrown away too quickly.

Air Cdre Henry Probert set the use of reservists and the disbandment of the RAuxAF in the context of Britain's post Imperial deployments which demanded that squadrons be able in the 50s and 60s to serve worldwide. **Ian Madelin** reflected on the Auxiliaries as centres for expansion in the 30s and suggested that such centres are of relevance in today's climate of retrenchment in the RAF itself. He agreed with **Alan Carlaw** that the US example of the National Guard and the USAF Reserve was relevant. The US Total Force Concept demonstrated a quite different attitude to reserves on the part of the USA.

Wg Cdr Peter Masterman brought the discussion back to Northern Skies, describing his service on Javelins, on 29 Sqn at Leuchars at the same time as Sir Peter Bairsto had served on No. 43 Squadron. At that time, it was always thought that Leuchars was too far North as a defensive base and his squadron regularly would fly South to Leconfield or Wattisham to hold two minute cockpit readiness. **Ian Madelin** and others confirmed that the Hunter squadrons would carry out similar migrations South, to Waterbeach and Horsham St. Faith. **Peter Masterman** reflected on his earlier experience on Canberras which would be ordered to fly at 30-35,000ft, to allow Meteors to engage them. **Ian Madelin** spoke of the psychological effect of preparing to engage Soviet aircraft with radar laid rear armament, especially when most interceptions would result in a stern attack down to 300 yards range.

Dennis Caldwell gave an amusing account of early attempt at what would later be known as Mixed Fighter Force tactics. The Hunters of 92 Sqn. and the Javelins of 33 Sqn. at Middleton St.

George trialled such tactics by day and night in the late 50s and it was concluded that although the aim of bringing more guns to bear on night bombers was a good one, the hazards involved were considerable. The trial was abandoned. Finally, **Peter Masterman** reflected on early difficulties with integrating fighter operations with Surface to Air Missiles. He had served at Patrington as a SAM controller for Bloodhound MkI squadrons in Yorkshire intended to protect the Thor IRBM squadrons of the Driffield Wing which was part of the strategic nuclear deterrent force. Squadrons were deployed at Breighton, Carnaby, Catfoss, Driffield and Full Sutton. Bloodhound squadrons were based at Carnaby and Breighton.

Professor Max Hammerton asked why it was that Britain and the Americans dropped the gun from fighters introduced at the end of the 50s. **Ian McBride** rehearsed the early history of the Lightning which originally had two guns with a further two as an option but all were removed to make space for a new instrument fit. It had not been properly recognised that early air to air missiles, on which all was staked, typically had a minimum range of around one mile. Below such ranges, ramming became the only option! The realisation of this deficiency (which had not been lost on the fighter pilot fraternity) came slowly, given that the threat to UK was from bombers armed with stand off missiles. However, with the emergence of a European tactical air threat in the wake of MC 14/3 and the doctrine of Flexible Response, the need to restore a gun capability was acted upon. Until the arrival of Tornado, the typical gun fit was a bolt-on modification.

Dennis Caldwell joined in the general excoriation of the later Lightning gun fit: in the Far East, the Australians were simply amazed that a gun should be mounted in a fuel tank, especially in an airframe with a known propensity to leak and to burst into flames. He spoke of early trials of air to air unguided missiles which provided some exciting moments for the then Flt Lt John Nicholls and were rumoured to continue rippling from the pack as it retracted into the fuselage! He touched on American decision making which linked the removal of the gun from the RF4 with a wish to ensure that recce pilots stuck to recce and were not tempted by the gun to play at being fighter pilots.

AVM Les Davis pursued the use of AAMs to counter a manned bomber threat, citing the American reliance on missiles for the F102 and F106 in the US continental air defence role. Only Vietnam brought the need for the gun to the fore. **Ian Madelin** followed this up with the reminder that some of the missiles employed in US air defence were nuclear-tipped. **Gp Capt Euan Black** spoke of two factors which militated against the use of the gun in the Lightning. Lamentable cockpit ergonomics and an inaccurate sighting system brought the gun into disrepute. By contrast, the Tornado F3 scores well on both counts. **Gp Capt David Hamilton** stressed the usefulness of the gun in peacekeeping operations.

The discussion moved into the area of the responsiveness of industry and the ability to exploit modifications introduced in short order. **Wg Cdr Andy Walton** pointed out how rapidly modifications had been achieved under the operational demands of, for example Bosnia, in contrast to the normally pedestrian rate of the peacetime procurement cycle spoken of by Ian Madelin.

David Hamilton spoke of the tremendous support for the RAF from industry at the time of the Gulf War but highlighted the difficulty of training crews to make best use of new kit introduced in short order. The risks involved in an 'alright on the night' philosophy were echoed by **Ian McBride** who said that it was only because there was sufficient time available for the Gulf War that many modifications were possible. As it was, some worthwhile modifications had to be done without, for the lack of time to train crews. The successes of the Gulf or the Falklands should not be allowed to justify parsimony in peacetime. **Euan Black** said that the RAF must never again accept an aircraft not ready for service. He took the first Tornados into Dhahran in August 1990 and the aircraft were not even capable of firing a head-on missile. They were quickly replaced but, with EFA on the horizon, the lessons must not be forgotten. Fleets within fleets must be avoided.

Sir Peter Bairsto made a powerful appeal for the RAF Historical Society to address itself to the issues of procurement in the post-war era. He cited the British propensity to produce magnificent flying machines with excellent engine/airframe combinations which were totally inadequate as integrated weapons systems. The Lightning was but one example of the weapon system being 'stuffed into an experimental aeroplane'. The repeated failure even to integrate adequate radios into fighter aircraft was a good example of the malaise.

John Baker-Cresswell brought the discussion back to the threat which had dominated the Defence of Northern Skies from the 50s to the 80s. Just how good had the potential opposition been, seen with benefit of the insights now made possible by the collapse of the

USSR? **David Hamilton** had been surprised to find how inefficient the Soviets had been. They had been sat upon by the communist system and discouraged from being innovative. That had fed through to their training which was very 'canned', just as for the Iraqi Air Force which based itself on Soviet ways. Soviet crews had the equipment and the basic skills but the quality of their training, the most important element, was lacking. He noted that the difficulty of persuading public and politicians alike of the need for hard training was a problem facing the RAF today, especially in an era of no direct threat, but one in which the Air Force is daily operating in some of the most exciting areas since the end of WWII. He also commented on the lack of sustainability of the MiG 29 which showed all the signs of having compromised reliability for greater sophistication.

Euan Black recounted how, after the fall of the Berlin Wall, the Luftwaffe had vetted a number of East German MiG 29 pilots and found them seriously below par in terms of training and performance in the air. He believed that, in the Cold War era, number counting was the dominant analyst's tool but that we had not actually looked discriminatingly at how well the opposition would operate. The Soviet Air Forces reminded him of the RAF of the 50s and 60s and had not progressed much beyond such levels.

A final question was asked about the RAF's operations at bases such as Leuchars and Leeming, in the Hardened Aircraft Shelters which had been built to make more robust the Northern air defences of the Cold War period. **Euan Black** spoke with some pride of the quality of these facilities which are probably the best ever provided. They also offer an ideal model for RAF squadrons to imitate when deployed to any part of the World as part of today's immediate reaction forces.

In drawing the session to a close, **Gp Capt Madelin** noted that discussion had, perforce, been limited to what Sir Peter Bairsto had earlier described as 'the worm's eye view'. He regretted that some of those responsible for designing the tactics and policies of the 50s and 60s – and which are now seen often to have been deeply flawed – had not been present to give an account of themselves!

Tornado F3 and Beyond

Chairman:

I am delighted to welcome Air Cdre Martin WIDDOWSON, the SASO at HQ 11 Gp, to bring the story right up to date. He is an experienced fighter pilot with service on Hunter, Lightning and Phantom under his belt and today has responsibilities in the air defence of the entire United Kingdom. He is very welcome as a representative of today's defenders of all UK skies.

The four years preceding my return to No. 11 Group as Senior Air Staff Officer only four months ago have seen momentous change. Starting with the fall of the Berlin Wall and the collapse of the Soviet Union, these years have seen a dramatic shift in the UK's military posture. Our forces have undergone a complete reorientation and have seen a new emphasis placed on readiness, as was highlighted only last week by the Secretary of State's announcements concerning Rapid Reaction Forces. In that sort of context, one must wonder which 'Northern Skies' we should be discussing today: the UK, the Adriatic or even the Gulf?

The rapid changes of the last few years have underscored the unpredictability of the World today. The UK has interests around the globe and we depend on a stable environment for our economic prosperity. Future attacks on our prosperity could take a number of forms, of which perhaps the most unlikely is that of a direct attack on the UK itself. Conflicts of the last 15 years, from the Falklands, through the Gulf to the former Yugoslavia have all involved our forces. We must be prepared for anything – anywhere!

The Government has defined three UK Defence Roles, each of which could involve our air defence forces. The protection of the UK and its dependent territories, even when there is no major threat, certainly does involve air defence. We continue to maintain two aircraft on alert, 24 hours a day, predominantly at the Northern AD base, RAF Leuchars in Fife. Our NATO role is to guard against a major threat to the UK or its allies. And the promotion of the UK's wider security interests through the maintenance of international peace and stability took our air defence units in the Gulf and, now, to the skies over Bosnia-Herzegovina.

To face these three challenges, we have forces spread widely throughout the UK but with the Cold War legacy of a bias to North and East. However, we continue to develop an impressive mobile capability which was put to the test in our speed of response to events in the Gulf and the Balkans. The Tornado F3 is in service North of the Humber at Leuchars and Leeming, and at Coninsby in Lincolnshire. The aircraft does not pretend to be an agile air superiority fighter and comparisons with aircraft such as the American F16 or F18, or with the Russian MiG 29 are unjust. It was designed as a long-range high speed interceptor against the Soviet Bomber threat. The ten years since it entered service have seen threats change considerably.

The F3 can fly at speeds up to Mach 2 and has an unrefuelled endurance of over four hours. Its AI radar offers an enormous improvement over that of the Phantom, giving target information at considerable ranges, including altitude, heading and formation disposition. It carries eight air to air missiles, four semi-active radar homing and four infra red guided. Its 27mm Mauser cannon may be used in air to air or air to ground mode. The flexibility offered by the strafe capability is retained because it is easier to maintain the capability than to have to attain it at a time of crisis. The aircraft carries flare and chaff self-protection kit. Two of the seven F3 squadrons are equipped with the very latest data link equipment, the Joint Tactical Information Distribution System, of JTIDS. This gives crews access to an unprecedented picture of the battle in the air. Information obtained by other sensors, such as other F3s or the E3-D

Airborne Early Warning (AEW) aircraft may be accessed. The F3 has not always had a good press and, although the aircraft is vastly better than at the time of its introduction, we look forward to the planned enhancement of its systems. (Note: this was confirmed by MoD in early 1996.)

Seven E3-D Sentry aircraft have been in service with No. 8 Sqn since 1991 and these are in constant demand for air and maritime surveillance and for air control. Its impressive twelve hour endurance can be extended by air to air refuelling and the aircraft also has JTIDS, making it in combination with Tornado F3 a very potent defensive system.

The strength of No. 11 Group also includes No. 100 Sqn, the Hawks of which are used to provide training for all operational elements of the Group. A further Hawk squadron would augment the Tornado F3 force in war. The training provided by No. 100 Sqn is of particular importance to the UK Air Defence Ground Environment – UKADGE – which has gone through an enormous programme of upgrading in recent years. Although not without problems, the result of this upgrading has been to create one of the most sophisticated Air Defence command and control systems in the world. The picture from all our radar sites is fed into the Integrated Command & Control System – ICCS – which enables commanders to deploy forces to best advantage. The sensors vary in quality but provide excellent coverage of the approaches to the UK. A future enhancement will feed the output of the main ATC radars into the system. We have recently regenerated a deployable tactical radar and control capability, No 1 Air Control Centre which is based at Boulmer. Although relatively unsophisticated at present, it should be the forerunner of a considerably enhanced system in the future.

Instability and weapon export proliferation make the prediction of potential threats almost impossible. Aircraft which could be ranged against us could as easily be of Western origin as from the former Soviet Union. The Mirage or the Fulcrum with short, medium or long range missiles could present real problems to RAF crews. Besides modern equipment, realistic and hard training are essential. A whole series of exercises and deployments test the fighter forces to the full, ranging from the North American 'Flag' series, to Far East deployments and exercising with Australian, Malaysian, New Zealand and Singaporean forces. Our home based air defence exercises offer superb air defence and battle management training, not only for the

RAF but for our European allies who participate by invitation. In the context of current operations, the need for such international training becomes essential and an indispensable aspect of our preparedness.

The list of overseas commitments – far removed from the Northern Skies of Leeming and Leuchars – is lengthy. Crews from 11 Group. squadrons man the air defences of the Falklands on rotation from UK bases. Tornado F3s have been deployed to Italy in support of Operation DENY FLIGHT since early 1993. At any time, eight aircraft and upwards of 200 air and ground crew personnel are at Gioia Del Colle. And the E3-D Sentry continues to play a major part in the airspace surveillance over Bosnia and in the direction of air assets in support of both UN and NATO operations.

For the future, the most immediate requirement is to enhance the capability of the Tornado F3 and to upgrade the UKADGE, both in terms of its radars and the command and control systems fed by them. The greater availability of JTIDS is high on any list of enhancements.

The longer term sees the biggest challenge of all, in the introduction of the Eurofighter 2000. This will be an agile, single seat, long range, multi-role aircraft with advanced long range missiles. Even at its present early stages of development, it is offering impressive technological advances and performance. We have every reason to believe that it will be a world beater. The EF 2000 and the E3-D Sentry together, and the modern UKADGE, will make a formidable UK air defence package – wherever we may have to deploy it.

Through a period of great change within the Royal Air Force and at a time when huge demands are being placed on them, our servicemen and women continue to deliver the goods. Despite all the inevitable worries and disturbance that are part of our present force reductions, they continue to show the most marvellous commitment – and excellence and quality in every aspect of their work. Northern Skies – and others – are in very good hands!

Concluding Remarks by AM Sir Frederick Sowrey

Chairman

I would now invite the Chairman of the RAF Historical Society Sir Freddie SOWREY to sum up. He is the fighter pilot son of the other Frederick Sowrey who downed a Zeppelin over Essex in 1916. He served during the war in fighter reconnaissance squadrons and, afterwards, served on and later commanded No 615 Sqn RAuxAF. He shares that honour with Wg Cdr Joe Kayll who commanded the same squadron in the Battles of France and Britain. Later, Sir Freddie commanded the first Javelin squadron, No 46 at RAF Odiham. He has wide experience of fighter operations and I am delighted to invite him to sum up our day.

In such an excellent day as this, all the presentations stand alone yet all knit together to form a composite whole. In summing-up I will try to pick out the threads of continuity and the truths that have survived over 80 years of Air Defence.

Ever since 1915 it is clear that however good your technology, and however skilled your personnel, air defence requires a system to cover time and three dimensional space. Such systems have been admirably described from the Ashmore plotting system through to the Dowding system of integrating all reporting sources to enable raids to be identified and tracked, and fighters controlled until the moment of interception. It was this tight control of resources and their best possible use which was the basis of victory in the Battle of Britain.

The geographical deployment of defensive systems has been

influenced by the areas and assets to be defended and the lines of approach of any attacking force:

1914-18

Initially coastal and naval targets all up the East Coast as well as the industrial centres. Following the Zeppelin raids on London, public pressure resulted in improved co-ordination between the elements of air defence to inflict unacceptable attrition on the subsequent Gotha raids from across the North Sea.

1939-45

The defence of industrial and political targets remained priority with the new addition of the security of our air defence system. The German occupation of French airfields was an unexpected (and unwelcome) development giving flexibility to their attacks.

Cold War

Policy developed through the protection of 'V' bomber airfields to providing sufficient early warning to get the deterrent force airborne before missile attack.

Throughout the day, stress had been laid on the need for equipment which was both reliable and effective. The modern thrust has been towards having your Early Warning and Control System actually airborne in AEW and using the increasing ranges of airborne intercept radars and 'fire and forget' weapons to make a 'kill' before the target is reached. Additionally, Air to Air refuelling has given operational options and a force multiplier previously unknown. And the ultimate success of any system will depend on its people – well trained, inventive and offensive in a defensive setting.

A tight defensive system has other advantages. The Germans were unsure of the actual 'D' Day landing areas partially because they were unable to fly successful photographic reconnaissance sorties over the embarkation areas of the South Coast. The achievement of defensive air supremacy will release resources for offensive effort. There is, of course, a reverse of this coin. Too great a concentration on defence will blunt offensive action – the Bomber Command offensive against Germany tied down Luftwaffe squadrons and Anti Aircraft Artillery which could have made a decisive impact on the Russian front.

So what of the future? I have already mentioned the trend towards having more of the reporting and control system in the air rather than on the ground. Satellites provide both early warning and reconnaissance capability – they are currently immune from interception and take their place in the ebb and flow of offence and defence. The availability of 'off the shelf' components for Ground Launched Cruise Missiles and the continual development of surface to surface missiles with Chemical Warfare or Bacteriological Warfare heads could give Third World countries a first class military capability. It is possible to envisage Air Defence coming the full circle and think again of the point defence of capital cities in Western Europe.

Thank you for being such receptive hosts to the RAF Historical Society which is dedicated to the accurate recording of lessons from the past. Thank you to all the speakers; thank you to the University and thank you to Air Vice-Marshal Sandy Hunter for the genesis and execution of a memorable day.